Dear Tina

The Chinese(?) book came out very well. I also published the enclosed book. You enjoyed reading some ideas from the Course in the past, so I thought you might like to read this introductory book that will give you a concise overview of the Course — with a mystical flavor.

Peace,
Don

38

An Overview of
"A Course in Miracles"

An Overview of
"*A Course in Miracles*"

≈ • ≈

Introduction to the Course—
What Beginners Need to Know

Donald James Giacobbe

Miracle Yoga Services

The overall cover design and interior layout of the text and graphics, including all the illustrations, were created by Donald James Giacobbe.

Published by Miracle Yoga Services
— miracleyoga@gmail.com —
Cottonwood, Arizona

Printed in the United States of America

BISAC Subject Codes and Headings:

OCC027510 Body, Mind, and Spirit: Spirituality—*A Course in Miracles*

OCC014000 Body, Mind & Spirit—New Thought

REL012120 Religion: Christian Life—Spiritual Growth

Library of Congress Control Number: 2011931552

Giacobbe, Donald James
An Overview of *A Course in Miracles*:
    Introduction to the Course—What Beginners Need to Know

ISBN 978-0-9843790-2-6

CONTENTS

≈ ◦ ≈

ABOUT THE AUTHOR

~ ◦ ~

Donald James Giacobbe recorded his life story in his autobiography, *Memory Walk in the Light*. He was employed for sixteen years as a case manager serving developmentally disabled clients. The professional nature of his work limited his ability to express his spiritual motivations overtly, so out of necessity he served as an "undercover agent" for God.

A more direct approach to spirituality was facilitated by living with Zen Buddhist seekers and then being part of a yoga community. Later he was the director of the Aquarian Age Yoga Center in Virginia Beach, VA. He served as an instructor of meditation and yoga, teaching college courses and appearing on television. He specialized in providing yoga teacher training certification courses and leading meditation workshops and retreats. Don has attempted in his teaching of meditation to strip away the rituals of Zen Buddhism and yoga practices and transpose only the bare essence into a Christian context. Techniques of meditation inspired by Eastern sources enhance the use of traditional Christian practices, such as the "Jesus Prayer," and lead to the overshadowing of the Holy Spirit that occurs in Christian contemplation. These techniques can be found in Don's book *Christian Meditation Inspired by Yoga and "A Course in Miracles": Opening to Divine Love in Contemplation*.

Don encourages the doing of God's Will, being receptive to the Holy Spirit, and finding Christ within the temple of one's own heart. While respecting all spiritual expressions, he became a monk by making his vow directly to God, without the stamp of approval from any religious organization. For many years Don used the term "Christian yoga" to describe his spiritual path, which combined following Christ with yoga disciplines. But in recent years he has adopted the term "Miracle Yoga" to describe the specific path of Christian yoga he has chosen. This form of spirituality is a synthesis of yoga and the philosophy of "A Course in Miracles," encouraging the seeker to see with "forgiving eyes" and to perceive Christ in everyone. Don's goal is to maintain a balance between opening to divine love inwardly and allowing that love to be extended outwardly to others.

PREFACE

~ ◦ ~

Imagine your friend tells you, "I'm studying *A Course in Miracles*, and it's transforming my life," and he gives you a copy of the 1249-page Course. You read some of it and tell your friend, "The Course has lofty ideas, but it's confusing, and I don't have time for something I don't really understand." Later your friend hands you a copy of *An Overview of "A Course in Miracles."* He says, "This will explain the Course in a nutshell. At least it will let you know why it's so inspiring for me, even if you don't want to study the Course yourself."

In this case, if your friend gives you this overview to express love without expecting anything in return, and if you lovingly receive his gift, this exchange of love is what the Course calls a "miracle." The Course is a unique synthesis of Eastern and Western philosophy containing profound psychological insights. The Course promises to bring peace to your mind and to teach you how to perform miracles in which you replace perceptions of fear with new perceptions of love and forgiveness. But at first the Course will bring you turmoil because you are giving up your customary way of viewing the world and yourself while at the same time attempting to absorb new and perplexing concepts.

When starting to read the Course, you may feel like you are putting together a complicated and frustrating jigsaw puzzle without having the benefit and reassurance of being able to see a clear picture of what the completed puzzle will look like. This overview will help you to step away from the intricate and puzzling details of the Course and to see the overall picture of the Course as a whole and where it is leading you. This book presents a clear and concise framework for interpreting and applying the unique Course principles. The seemingly separate spiritual principles in the Course are actually totally interrelated and fit together like the pieces of a jigsaw puzzle to accomplish a single unified purpose, which will bring inner peace and purposefulness to your life. Through application, you will see how these ideas work together toward the one goal of integrating and unifying the mind. Reading this overview will provide you with enough information to make an informed decision on whether or not to proceed with an in-depth study of the Course itself that will enable you to apply its spiritual principles to your everyday experiences and especially to improving your personal relationships.

ACKNOWLEDGMENTS

~ o ~

I am very grateful for the support, suggestions, encouragement, and proofreading of my sister Lillian Blackburn. I appreciate Tom Dunn, Nancy Bonfield, and Shirley Bessette for serving as proofreaders. My thanks go to Chris Gibbons for his copy editing assistance.

INTRODUCTION

~ ○ ~

A Course in Miracles teaches that problems and outer circumstances in the world do not determine your peace of mind. The peace of Christ is already within you, waiting only for your recognition of its presence. Whether or not you gain access to this inner peace is up to you. You can set aside quiet times every day for meditation to become aware of the divine presence and the inner peace this presence brings. However, even if you do practice meditation, the Course maintains that there is more that you need to do to find peace in the outer world of form. You are responsible for the decisions that bring either the perceptions of peace or the perceptions of turmoil to your mind. Yet how can you make choices that will bring peace to you in the midst of the challenging occurrences of life? You can find peace of mind no matter what is happening in your life by changing your thinking from perceptions of fear to perceptions of love and forgiveness. The Course provides a practical means for learning this lesson of changing perceptions with the goal of obtaining peace of mind. It's called *A Course in Miracles* because it trains the mind to perform "miracles," which are changes in perception that manifest love instead of fear. The Course places a great deal of emphasis on your relationships with others and how others can help you to grow spiritually.

The Course integrates the ideas of Eastern philosophy into a Western context that can be applied by Christians of any denomination or even by seekers who have no formal or informal affiliation with Christ. In addition to being inclusive of Eastern philosophy, the Course mixes in a profound understanding of psychology from a spiritual perspective. This unique synthesis of Eastern and Western philosophy and theology with psychology has attracted a growing number of spiritual seekers. From its initial publication in 1976, it has had an amazing growth spurt with no initial advertising. The Course presents many familiar spiritual concepts but explains them in a very systematic and complete way. For example, concepts of the ego as the false self and your true nature as the true Self can be found in Eastern philosophy. However, the Course presents these concepts in a Western context that greatly expands the psychological understanding of these ideas.

In addition to these familiar concepts, the Course has transformed many lives with its unique ideas that do not neatly fit into any standard spiritual model. These ideas are so unusual that at first they are difficult to comprehend. Also, newcomers are often intimidated by the sheer size of the Course because it is 1249 pages that are presented in three volumes. A beginner might welcome the aim of the Course to retrain the mind for the purpose of "...removing the blocks to the awareness of love's presence."[1] A newcomer may even attend Course study groups, which are grassroots meetings that are always free and open to anyone. Yet after reading the first 100 pages of the Course, this same beginner may suffer "information overdose," producing more questions than answers. "To learn this course requires willingness to question every value that you hold."[2] The Course is long and involves introspection and intensive soul-searching, so it can be disorienting. A typical beginner does not have a framework for understanding the Course as a whole and so does not know where all this new and confusing information is leading. A traveler must have a clear picture of the itinerary and the final arrival point before being willing to make the entire journey to an unfamiliar destination. Similarly, a beginner must have a clear picture of how all the parts of the Course fit together and an understanding of its benefits in order to invest the time and effort needed to study and apply its spiritual principles. This economical book is an overview designed to meet this need by providing clarity to the beginner, helping him understand the distinctive spiritual principles of the Course and how these are all aimed toward the single goal of bringing healing and wholeness to the mind.

The first eighty pages of this book provide a clear and comprehensive framework for studying the Course as a means of integrating and unifying the mind. While reading this overview, please pay particular attention to the words that are set apart with bold letters to indicate they are key terms used in the Course. In some cases these are familiar words, but the Course has given them new meanings. To help you review and recall the basic ideas that are introduced in the main body of this overview, there are two very brief summaries of the Course at the end of this book. The first summary is a six-page section consisting of fourteen questions and answers taken directly from Course quotations. The second summary is a three-page list of fourteen unique ideas that distinguish the Course from other thought systems.

Yet the Course is more than just a collection of unusual ideas. As an analogy, you can think of the Course as being like a tree. Beginners initially become overly focused on seeing and examining only the leaves, which represent the numerous and often perplexing ideas in the Course. This overview helps the beginner notice the branches, which symbolize how the Course ideas are interrelated and how they apply to everyday life. In addition, this book reminds the beginner about the trunk, which is the one Source of all Course concepts. The point of this analogy is that the Course is many-faceted like the leaves, but all the various ideas of the Course are totally interconnected and directed toward a single purpose. Through application, these ideas work together toward the one goal of integrating and unifying the mind. If you study the Course, your purpose will be to heal your own mind. Studying the Course will lead you from the ideas (the leaves) back to the interrelationships and applications of the ideas (the branches) and finally back to the Source (the trunk).

What is this Source? Yes, it is God, your Creator. But this Source is also your own true nature in God, which is your true Self. The healing the Course offers to your mind is an acceptance of who you really are. This healing brings wholeness to the mind and a new way of thinking and navigating through the world. Since your true nature is love, you heal and unify the mind through replacing fearful perceptions with loving perceptions. This process of transformation will ultimately and inevitably lead to your final destiny—the joyous delight of awakening in Heaven.

Now let's carry the tree analogy one step further. When you look at a tree, the part you don't see is the roots that nourish the tree. The roots symbolize all the unseen spiritual influences that nourish you, the most important being the Holy Spirit and Jesus. If you decide to take this transforming path of consciously uncovering who you are, you have the assurance from the Course that the Holy Spirit will guide you every step of the way, and Jesus Himself will walk with you.

> ... this course was sent to open up the path of light to us, and teach us, step by step, how to return to the eternal Self we thought we lost.
> I [Jesus] take the journey with you. For I share your doubts and fears a little while, that you may come to me who recognize the road by which all fears and doubts are overcome. We walk together.[3]

Although this overview is necessarily concise, it provides a framework for understanding the Course without diluting its inspirational message. Nevertheless, an overview cannot be the whole story, just as listening to only part of a symphony will not replace becoming immersed in hearing an entire symphony. Benefiting from the Course requires understanding, followed by appreciation, leading to application. Reading this overview will provide you with enough information to make an informed decision on whether or not to proceed with an in-depth study of the Course itself that will enable you to apply its spiritual principles to your daily life.

Why Study the Course?

~ o ~

My happiest childhood days were spent with my friends on sunny summer days at the beach. The older children were able to swim out to the deep water and dive off a large wooden raft anchored offshore. At first, I was a cautious swimmer, slowly wading one step at a time into the intimidating cold ocean water before finally jumping in. That's how most beginners apprehensively dabble in *A Course in Miracles* without jumping into it wholeheartedly. Many beginners say they are familiar with the Course, yet they cannot provide even an elementary summary of its contents. Typically a beginner might describe the Course as a "philosophy of love." Nevertheless, the Course is not primarily about love. Rather, it enables love to manifest. And the Course is not primarily a philosophy because it focuses on application rather than theory.

The Course acts in the very personal and challenging way a doctor would giving you bad news and good news. The bad news in the Course is that your thought system is very unhealthy now. The good news is that the Course offers you a new thought system as a remedy that will restore your mind to good health. But will you take the remedy just as it is prescribed? Well, that depends on whether or not you are willing to understand and apply the remedy.

The subtitle of this overview is "Introduction to the Course— What Beginners Need to Know" because it provides the basic concepts needed to understand the Course. The first and most crucial thing you need to know as a beginner is: *What you have taught yourself about the world and even about yourself is quite inaccurate.* You will need to recognize how unhealthy your current condition is, since that will be your motivation for learning about the remedy provided by the Course and how to apply it. Possibly you have taught yourself to acquire a "healthy self-image." By worldly standards, this is a very commendable accomplishment, undoubtedly much better than learning to adopt an unhealthy self-image. The problem is that *any* self-image you have given yourself—good or bad—cannot tell you who you really are. The sobering truth is that you are not qualified to define yourself. Only your Creator has the authority and wisdom to define you. The Course is designed to teach you how to understand your Creator's definition of you and how to apply that definition to your daily life. The Course is a preparation for the ultimate happy surprise of *directly experiencing* who you are.

Unfortunately, you may be reluctant to accept that your mind is currently so unhealthy that you do not even know who you are in reality. If you remain steadfastly reluctant to let go of what you have taught yourself about life and about yourself, you will only timidly get your feet wet, and not want to dive headlong into the Course. But total commitment to the Course is not required in the beginning in order to benefit from it. Just as taking baby steps into the water helps you become acclimated to the cold water of the ocean, easing your way into the study of the Course helps you to become acclimated to it. The Course anticipates your resistance to it and offers you the following advice for starting to practice its lessons:

> Some of the ideas the workbook presents you will find hard to believe, and others may seem to be quite startling. This does not matter. You are merely asked to apply the ideas as you are directed to do. You are not asked to judge them at all. You are asked only to use them. It is their use that will give them meaning to you, and will show you that they are true.
>
> Remember only this; you need not believe the ideas, you need not accept them, and you need not even welcome them. Some of them you may actively resist. None of this will matter, or decrease their efficacy. But do not allow yourself to make exceptions in applying the ideas the workbook contains, and whatever your reactions to the ideas may be, use them. Nothing more than that is required.[4]

By studying and consistently applying the Course principles, you can overcome your resistance and come to a place of acceptance, which will allow you to become an enthusiastic student. Similar to the way the ocean cannot be fully appreciated until you entirely submerge yourself in it, the Course cannot be fully appreciated until you delve into it wholeheartedly without reservation. You will not fully invest in the remedy the Course offers until you gradually become convinced of its value and how much you need it to bring healing to your mind.

The Course is an instruction manual that teaches you how to live in accordance with who you are. The basic premise is that who you think you are needs to change in order to accept who you are in reality. Who you think you are needs to learn through *subtraction* and *addition*: First, through subtraction you learn how to unlearn what you have taught yourself. Second, through addition you learn how to accept your true Identity. This process of subtraction and addition is the remedy the Course offers to heal your mind. This remedy can be summarized in one word: **forgiveness**.

The central message of the Course is forgiveness because it contains in itself both ways of learning. The subtraction aspect of forgiveness allows you to let go of your current judgments and limited perspective. The addition aspect of forgiveness provides you with a means of healing your mind through a new vision of the world, of your brothers and sisters, and of yourself. Helping you gain this healing vision is the aim of studying the Course, which has three parts: The **Text** sets out the philosophical basis for the Course. The **Workbook for Students** provides daily lessons for one year so you can put the spiritual principles of the Course into practical application. The **Manual for Teachers** provides instruction in how to proceed with your life after studying the Course principles and completing the Workbook lessons.

The teachings of the Course are a unique combination of an inspiring Christian theology and the lofty insights of Eastern philosophy, as well as a profound understanding of modern psychology. Western spirituality is primarily focused on loving interpersonal relationships and forgiveness. Eastern spirituality is mainly about the individual seeker's relationship with the divine and is concerned with inward seeking that brings about spiritual awakening. Various Course scholars and Course organizations will present slightly different interpretations of the Course. The majority of these interpretations highlight Western spirituality and place much less emphasis on Eastern spirituality. Unlike a typical Course summary, the overview you are reading now offers an equal emphasis on Western forgiveness and Eastern awakening and also focuses on experiencing the inner light and love that facilitates both forgiveness and awakening.

The long-term goal of all spiritual seeking is the ultimate awakening sought in the East, while the short-term goal used in the West is forgiveness as the means to grow toward that awakening. The Course centers on the short-term goal of forgiveness, but to put forgiveness into practical application requires keeping the long-term goal of divine awakening in your awareness. This means implementing a new kind of forgiveness that affirms seeing the divine here and now in the world of time and space. Thus forgiveness involves giving up the way you normally perceive the world and replacing it with a new way of perceiving. This giving up of the old way of seeing and accepting a radically new way of seeing is illustrated in what could be called the "horse-of-a-different-color" analogy:

Imagine that you are given a stack of photographs of horses. Each snapshot is taken from a different angle. Each horse in each photo has a different characteristic color. You learn from a friend that one specific photo was taken with a camera that had a colored filter that distorted the picture. Next you generalize your learning by realizing that all the photos are distorted images that do not accurately reflect the reality of the subject matter. From your friend you accept a plan to correct all the distortions by using your friend's gift of a photo editing program. After scanning the photos into your computer and using this photo editing program, you change the photos to a black and white format. The black and white photos are still a distortion of the subject matter, but they more closely reflect the reality of the horse than the colored distortions. As you gaze at the pictures, you overlook all the black and grey parts of the background, and you look only at the white image of the horse. After looking at several pictures, you generalize your learning and realize something surprising: The photos were not of different horses; they were actually all pictures of the *same* horse, a perfectly white horse. Then, after looking at a very clear close-up photo of the white face of the horse, you remember that this is a white horse owned by your friend. To confirm your memory, your friend shows you his real white horse that had been depicted in the photographs. You can see how beautiful the actual living horse is in contrast to the two-dimensional photos that are merely lifeless images. Finally you embrace the white horse itself.

Using this analogy, your body's eyes are like a camera that takes pictures of this world, showing many different forms. According to the Course, this is "image making" that deceives you. The Course teachings act like the photo editing program in the horse analogy to help you set aside your image making and see in a new way, without distortion. Looking past the apparently different images of objects and people, you can learn how to perceive the underlying **oneness** that has been hidden. This new kind of perception that sees the truth beyond outer appearances is called "real vision," "the Holy Spirit's vision," or **"Christ's vision,"** and will be elaborated upon subsequently.

That is one interpretation of the horse analogy. Here is another interpretation: Christ's vision and many other true perceptions in the Course appear at first glance to be distinctly different spiritual principles, like the colored photos in the horse analogy. After reading this overview, however, you will see that these seemingly different spiritual concepts are completely interrelated and are all moving in just one coordinated direction. They form an entirely unified thought system, expressing just "*one* meaning, *one* emotion and *one* purpose."[5] The Course maintains that this single purpose is *your* one purpose, and it motivates *your* one function in the world. What is this one purpose and one function that you have but may not yet recognize? Before answering that question, you must first identify the obstacles that prevent you from seeing the world as it really is and that obscure its single meaning.

Obstacles to Correct Perception

~ • ~

Let's start by considering the world of time and space. Because of the passing of time, the world is a place in which everything is changing, is temporary, and is the inevitable result of what has occurred in the past, producing the current state of affairs. In terms of space, everything in this world is limited to one particular space, is the product of all the other forms and forces acting upon it, and is defined by its separation in space from all other forms.

"Look at the world, and you will see nothing attached to anything beyond itself. All seeming entities can come a little nearer, or go a little farther off, but cannot join."[6]

Since it is a world in which every object and every person is separate, it is a place where isolated and alienated people live their lives of quiet, or not so quiet, desperation. Everyone has a separate identity called the **ego**. The ego seeks to inflate self-worth by seeking **specialness** through being better than others. Some people engage in a limited number of **special hate relationships** in which each partner seeks specialness by hating and attacking the other. Most people form **special love relationships** in which love becomes reduced to a **bargain**. In this relationship bargain, **giving to get** becomes a way of life. Each partner gives his specialness to the other, but only to get more specialness in return. They surround themselves with **idols** that increase their sense of specialness, such as possessions, money, power, social status, talents, accomplishments, and association with special people who have special attributes.

But the acquisition of specialness is always at the expense of others that are seen as less special. Therefore, seeking specialness is a form of selfishness because others must lose so you can gain specialness. The selfishness in seeking specialness involves the concept of **sin**. The typical understanding of the word "sin" is that it is an attack, since it is a violation of someone or something so you can gain some benefit for yourself. Because sin violates others, it produces fear and the uneasy or even painful feeling of **guilt**. Thus there must be a way of hiding all this seeking of specialness from others and from yourself so you will have the appearance of goodness. Hiding the seeking of specialness is accomplished quite easily through the ego manufacturing the most superficial self-concept, which the Course calls the "**face of innocence.**"

> The concept of the self the world would teach is not the thing that it appears to be. For it is made to serve two purposes, but one of which the mind can recognize. The first presents the face of innocence, the aspect acted on. It is this face that smiles and charms and even seems to love. It searches for companions and it looks, at times with pity, on the suffering, and sometimes offers solace. It believes that it is good within an evil world.
>
> This aspect can grow angry, for the world is wicked and unable to provide the love and shelter innocence deserves. And so this face is often wet with tears at the injustices the world accords to those who would be generous and good. This aspect never makes the first attack. But every day a hundred little things make small assaults upon its innocence, provoking it to irritation, and at last to open insult and abuse.
>
> The face of innocence the concept of the self so proudly wears can tolerate attack in self-defense, for is it not a well-known fact the world deals harshly with defenseless innocence? No one who makes a picture of himself omits this face, for he has need of it. The other side he does not want to see. Yet it is here the learning of the world has set its sights, for it is here the world's "reality" is set, to see to it the idol lasts.[7]

Think of when you go on a job interview. How you present yourself in that situation is your face of innocence because it is the concept of yourself the world has taught you to put on display. It has the purpose of presenting you in your best light, and the purpose also of hiding the darker side of your nature. Your face of innocence says, "I am a good person. I go along with my life, doing the best I can to mind my own affairs and meet all my needs while accomplishing all the tasks required of me. Hopefully no one or nothing in the world will get in my way. I try to be kind and giving and even forgiving, but, of course, there are limitations on how far I can go with my kindness without being taken advantage of by others who may not appreciate me. The world is such a difficult place that sometimes others do take advantage of me. Then I am compelled to stand up for myself. Sometimes I even have to attack others, but actually I am just defending myself in response to what others have done to me first, so I am justified in my actions." Does this description of the face of innocence sound familiar? It should, because it is the universal face of innocence that is a one-size-fits-all mask and remarkably useful self-image fully utilized by everyone on the planet. It preserves your internal sense of goodness while allowing you to seek specialness. Thus you can engage in all sorts of attacks and feel fully justified without acknowledging any sin or guilt on your part.

If it is hard for you to admit that you wear the face of innocence, it will be even harder to admit that there are two more masks that are hidden within you, mostly beyond your conscious awareness. If you look carefully below the face of innocence, you will perceive that there is the mask of the **victim**, who has been victimized by others or by the all-pervading forces of the world. Then you will also see that below the victim mask, there is the mask of the **victimizer**, who has apparently been forced into the role of being the attacker in response to first being attacked by others.

The masks of the face of innocence, the victim, and the victimizer are all necessary to provide **self-justification**, which is needed as a means of avoiding the uneasy inner feeling of guilt. Guilt is the feeling enkindled in us when we feel we have sinned. Sin is attack. It is a violation of others or a violation of goodness or even a violation of God Himself. Guilt is so uncomfortable that it must be denied and projected away, preferably onto others who we decide deserve it. **Denial** and **projection** seem to get rid of guilt and are used for that purpose. Instead, denial and projection only result in increasing your inner sense of guilt. Guilt is sometimes projected onto one's own body and later manifests as **sickness**, without the sick person recognizing self-imposed guilt as the cause.

What Has the God of Love Created?

~ o ~

In the process of identifying the previously mentioned obstacles to perception, you can see a dark picture of the world that shows it as a place of separation, self-deception, fear, pain, guilt, sin, and evil. Every traditional Christian theology agrees that "God is Love." So what has the God of Love created? Most Christians would say that God created this world, but how could a God of Love create a place filled with so much miserable darkness, suffering, and evil in it? Most Christians also say that God has provided a place called hell, where all the unrepentant evil doers will go to spend eternity. Traditional Christians supply many justifications that skeptical observers could claim give God Himself "a divine face of innocence." In such a belief system, many justifications are necessary to explain why God allows evil in the world. Additional justifications are needed to explain how a God of Love is still loving while His justice demands that there must be a hell for all unrepentant, evil-minded sinners to burn for eternity. On the other hand, many disenchanted Christians reasonably conclude that God is not a God of Unconditional Love, and so in their disillusionment they give up religion altogether.

Here is where the Course departs from every other Christian belief system. The Course agrees that God is Love, but offers the radical idea that God did not make this world and that there is no hell, where souls suffer for eternity. Consequently, we must return to the original question: "So what has the God of Love created?" Everything in the Course rests upon the answer to this question. The answer is: *God created you.* You probably agree, but wait a minute. Here is what the Course says you believe about yourself when you take off your face of innocence and all your masks:

> You think you are the home of evil, darkness and sin. You think if anyone could see the truth about you he would be repelled, recoiling from you as if from a poisonous snake. You think if what is true about you were revealed to you, you would be struck with horror so intense that you would rush to death by your own hand, living on after seeing this being impossible.[8]

This quotation brings up the same problem as before. If you are a sinner, how could the God of Love create a sinner? The answer is that God did indeed create you, but you are not a sinner because God did not create you as a sinner. "These weird beliefs [in your sinfulness] He does not share with you."[9] God could create only like Himself. "You *are* as God created you, and so is *every* living thing you look upon, regardless of the images you see."[10] Understanding how God created you like Himself requires you to give up all the many thoughts of limitation that you have laid upon yourself.

> Salvation requires the acceptance of but one thought;— you are as God created you, not what you made of yourself. Whatever evil you may think you did, you are as God created you. Whatever mistakes you made, the truth about you is unchanged. Creation is eternal and unalterable. Your sinlessness is guaranteed by God. You are and will forever be exactly as you were created. Light and joy and peace abide in you because God put them there.[11]

God created you as an extension of His Love because God's only function is to share all of Himself—to share all of His reality, His joy, His eternity, His infinity, His holiness, and all His very Being. The only thing God cannot share is His place as the First Cause. "To create is to love. Love extends outward simply because it cannot be contained. Being limitless it does not stop. It creates forever, but not in time."[12] God created you and gave His Love to you as your own true nature. His Love is just one thing, one unity, and His Love is transcendent.

> Perhaps you think that different kinds of love are possible. Perhaps you think there is a kind of love for this, a kind for that; a way of loving one, another way of loving still another. Love is one. It has no separate parts and no degrees; no kinds nor levels, no divergencies and no distinctions. It is like itself, unchanged throughout. It never alters with a person or a circumstance. It is the Heart of God, and also of His Son.
> Love's meaning is obscure to anyone who thinks that love can change.[13]

Creation is **extension**, so what is created is extended from God. Creation is part of God Himself. God extends by sharing His Thoughts, and the Course maintains, "Ideas leave not their source."[14] Thus what is created never leaves God Who is the eternal Source.

God created His Sons by extending His Thought, and retaining the extensions of His Thought in His Mind. All His Thoughts are thus perfectly united within themselves and with each other. The Holy Spirit enables you to perceive this wholeness *now*. God created you to create. You cannot extend His Kingdom until you know of its wholeness.

Thoughts begin in the mind of the thinker, from which they reach outward. This is as true of God's Thinking as it is of yours.[15]

The Course offers a paradox when it identifies one Son and many Sons. The **one Son** is the **Christ**. But this one Christ has many **parts**, who are the many Sons that make up the **Sonship** of Christ. You are a single part of the one Christ, and so you are one of the Sons of God. The paradox is that every part contains the whole Christ: "...all of God's Sons are of equal value, and their equality is their oneness. The whole power of God is in every part of Him...."[16]

Every part of the one Christ possesses the awareness of reality. This awareness is called **knowledge**, and every part has all of this knowledge. However, knowledge, which is total awareness, has nothing to do with the partial awareness of **perception**, which is the means of thinking in the world of form.

The very real difference between perception and knowledge becomes quite apparent if you consider this: There is nothing partial about knowledge. Every aspect is whole, and therefore no aspect is separate. You are an aspect of knowledge, being in the Mind of God, Who knows you. All knowledge must be yours, for in you is all knowledge. Perception, at its loftiest, is never complete.[17]

Because you rely on perception in this world, you do not and cannot fully understand the paradox of how every part of Christ can contain the whole of Christ. After all, perception says that the whole is a collection of parts, and that parts are only parts.

The whole does define the part, but the part does not define the whole [when using perception]. Yet [when using knowledge] to know in part is to know entirely because of the fundamental difference between knowledge and perception. In perception the whole is built up of parts that can separate and reassemble in different constellations. But knowledge never changes, so its constellation is permanent. The idea of part-whole relationships has meaning only at the level of perception, where change is possible. Otherwise, there is no difference between the part and whole [in the total awareness of knowledge].[18]

As part of Christ, you live in God, in reality, in oneness, in the place or rather the condition called **Heaven**, which transcends time and the forms of space.

There is no life outside of Heaven. Where God created life, there life must be. In any state apart from Heaven life is illusion. At best it seems like life; at worst, like death. Yet both are judgments on what is not life, equal in their inaccuracy and lack of meaning. Life not in Heaven is impossible, and what is not in Heaven is not anywhere. Outside of Heaven, only the conflict of illusion stands; senseless, impossible and beyond all reason, and yet perceived as an eternal barrier to Heaven. Illusions are but forms. Their content is never true.[19]

The Separation

≈ ० ≈

Now the obvious question you may ask is: "How did I get here in this world of time and space?" As strange as it sounds, you are still right now in Heaven, and you are still as God created you as part of Himself. But you have lost your awareness of being in Heaven. Losing the peace of Heaven was the result of some parts of the one Christ asking God for "special favor."

> You were at peace until you asked for special favor. And God did not give it for the request was alien to Him, and you could not ask this of a Father Who truly loved His Son. Therefore you made of Him an unloving father, demanding of Him what only such a father could give. And the peace of God's Son was shattered, for he no longer understood his Father.[20]

The parts of Christ that did not get "special favor" (special love) from God chose to cut off their direct communication with God. They could not really separate themselves from God, but they could severely limit their awareness of Him. Therefore, they decided to fall asleep in Heaven and to have a *collective dream* that could be called the "collusion illusion." Thus these parts made what the Course refers to as **the separation**. The dreaming parts made a dream world by manufacturing space and time. They projected a small portion of their awareness into individual bodies. The love, holiness, joy, and unlimited unifying expansiveness of Heaven were replaced by dreams of fear, depression, guilt, and the limitations of separation. The unlimited awareness of knowledge in Heaven was replaced by the limited awareness of perception. The device that made all these illusions possible was the individual ego, which is the concept of a separate and self-sufficient self.

> When God created you He made you part of Him. That is why attack within the Kingdom is impossible. You made the ego without love, and so it does not love you. You could not remain within the Kingdom without love, and since the Kingdom *is* love, you believe that you are without it. This enables the ego to regard itself as separate and outside its maker, thus speaking for the part of your mind that believes *you* are separate and outside the Mind of God.[21]

You are not outside the Kingdom, not outside Heaven, but the ego makes you think you are separate and have really left God. In fact, you are only indulging in a fantasy that has no reality at all. At first, it may seem like just an interesting theoretical idea that everything in the world of form is merely an illusion, a psychological trick of the mind, fabricated by the ego. Yet careful reflection can lead you to see that the illusory nature of the world provides you with a transforming power. If all the limitations of the world were real, there would be no way of overcoming them. However, because they are merely a dream, you, like Dorothy in the *Wizard of OZ*, have the power within you to wake up from your dream and go Home. This is the liberating central message of the Course, repeatedly reminding you that you remain just as loving and guiltless as when God created you in eternity.

Nevertheless, you cannot actually wake up by yourself alone for the simple reason that you are not alone. "The ego's voice is an hallucination. You cannot expect it to say 'I am not real.' Yet you are not asked to dispel your hallucinations alone."[22] Because perception is so limited and alien to knowledge, you need help to return to the knowledge that would allow you to wake up from your dream of separation. Graciously your loving Father responded at the instant of the separation by creating a whole new extension of Himself, called the **Holy Spirit**, to be your means of awakening.

> The Holy Spirit is the Mediator between the interpretations of the ego and the knowledge of the spirit. His ability to deal with symbols enables Him to work with the ego's beliefs in its own language. His ability to look beyond symbols into eternity enables Him to understand the laws of God, for which He speaks. He can therefore perform the function of reinterpreting what the ego makes, not by destruction but by understanding. Understanding is light, and light leads to knowledge. The Holy Spirit is in light because He is in you who are light, but you yourself do not know this. It is therefore the task of the Holy Spirit to reinterpret you on behalf of God.
>
> You cannot understand yourself alone. This is because you have no meaning apart from your rightful place in the Sonship, and the rightful place of the Sonship is God. This is your life, your eternity and your Self. It is of this that the Holy Spirit reminds you. It is this that the Holy Spirit sees. This vision frightens the ego because it is so calm.[23]

After the separation your mind became split. "The separation is merely another term for a split mind."[24] Your whole mind with knowledge in Heaven became a **split mind** with the acceptance of perception. "Perception is based on a separated state, so that anyone who perceives at all needs healing."[25] Awakening from your dream requires the healing of your split mind so that it becomes whole again. Your split mind has one portion ruled by the ego and another portion where the Holy Spirit resides. The split mind is maintained by keeping these two parts of the mind apart from each other. This separation of the mind is supported by a disordered mental process called **dissociation**, which the Course describes in this way:

> Dissociation is a distorted process of thinking whereby two systems of belief which cannot coexist are both maintained. If they are brought together, their joint acceptance becomes impossible. But if one is kept in darkness from the other, their separation seems to keep them both alive and equal in their reality. Their joining thus becomes the source of fear, for if they meet, acceptance must be withdrawn from one of them. You cannot have them both, for each denies the other. Apart, this fact is lost from sight, for each in a separate place can be endowed with firm belief. Bring them together, and the fact of their complete incompatibility is instantly apparent. One will go, because the other is seen in the same place.[26]

Because you currently identify with your ego and accept its thought system as your own, you believe in illusions that do not reflect your true nature. Dissociation allows you to be in denial of the other part of your split mind that is the home of the Holy Spirit. The purpose of the Course is to help you learn how to let go of your denial and to accept the thought system offered to you by the Holy Spirit. Your denial is so strong that overcoming it is a very gradual process in which you accept individual loving perceptions from the Holy Spirit one at a time.

What happens to the ego's thought system when you accept a loving thought from the Holy Spirit? The above quotation provides the answer. If the perceptions from two dissociated thought systems are brought together, their contradictory nature becomes very obvious. Therefore, when you accept the belief in a loving perception from the Holy Spirit's thought system, a corresponding fearful thought from the ego's thought system would be clearly identified as mutually exclusive. Seeing this contradictory nature of the two thoughts, you could only believe in one of them. With the help of the Holy Spirit, you would always choose to keep the loving thought and release the fearful thought. This is because the reality of love overcomes the unreality of fear, just as darkness always disappears in the presence of light.

This explains why each time you acquire a loving perception, you will automatically let go of an incompatible fearful perception of the ego. Learning to accept loving perceptions helps you to strengthen your identification with your true nature and weaken your identification with the ego. As you accept loving perceptions, you are opening to your own true nature of love. As you release unloving perceptions, you are releasing fear that originates from identification with the ego. Accepting love fosters union and releases fear and separation. Thus the healing of your split mind is a collaborative venture in which you join with others for the purpose of healing. The process of replacing fear with love is what happens in practicing forgiveness in which you heal your own split mind as you offer the miracle of healing to others.

There are different levels of perception in your split mind. Below the face of innocence, below the victim mask, and below the victimizer mask in your mind is the **call for love**, which is the part of your mind that is in pain and calls out for help. Below the call for love is your **right mind**, which is also called the **real world**, a place of only loving perception. Below the real world is the **Christ Mind**, which is still filled with knowledge although you have lost your access to that total awareness. The Holy Spirit has the unique role of having one foot in perception and one foot in knowledge, so He resides simultaneously in both the real world of loving perception and in the Christ Mind of knowledge. The function of the Holy Spirit is to heal your split mind if you provide Him with the opportunity to do so. Your task is to bring the darkness in the ego's part of your mind to the Holy Spirit and allow His light to heal your split mind.

> The Holy Spirit asks of you but this; bring to Him every secret you have locked away from Him. Open every door to Him, and bid Him enter the darkness and lighten it away. At your request He enters gladly. He brings the light to darkness if you make the darkness open to Him. But what you hide He cannot look upon. He sees for you, and unless you look with Him He cannot see. The vision of Christ is not for Him alone, but for Him with you. Bring, therefore, all your dark and secret thoughts to Him, and look upon them with Him. He holds the light, and you the darkness. They cannot coexist when both of You together look on them. His judgment must prevail, and He will give it to you as you join your perception to His.[27]

Wrong-mindedness and Right-mindedness

~ • ~

Your perceptions can be **true perceptions**, which are loving, or **false perceptions**, which are unloving. False perceptions, produced by listening to the ego, induce fear and involve **wrong-mindedness**. The terms described previously such as special hate relationships, special love relationships, bargaining, giving to get, seeking specialness, acquiring idols, the face of innocence, the victim mask, the victimizer mask, denial, projection, and sickness are all examples of the faulty use of the mind that is called wrong-mindedness. This listening to the ego involves perceiving fear, anger, sin, guilt, disease, and death as if they were real. But the ego and its wrong-mindedness can only make illusions *seem* real. Although you can and do make illusions, your saving grace is that God cannot produce illusions and does not recognize the slightest bit of reality in them. With God you can and do participate in reality in Heaven, but apart from God you cannot produce reality or even alter your changeless reality by making illusions. The New Age saying, "You create your own reality," is not true. In truth, "You create your own unreality," although the Course would say, "You *make* your own unreality," since *creating* is a divine activity of pure love.

Are you willing to admit God is right about you and you are wrong about yourself? Let's suppose you are willing to admit your mistaken perception and want to change your thinking. In this case, the Holy Spirit asks you to give Him "**your little willingness**."[28] Ultimately the Holy Spirit wants you to wake up in Heaven because that is what you also truly want. The Holy Spirit has established the **Atonement**, which is His plan for salvation and which is the correction of all your mistakes and all their effects. However, He turns your attention toward interim goals that will eventually lead to awakening. Since you made the dream of the world, you are not a victim of the world. The Holy Spirit reminds you that even now you are totally responsible for how you *experience* the world.

This is the only thing that you need do for vision, happiness, release from pain and the complete escape from sin, all to be given you. Say only this, but mean it with no reservations, for here the power of salvation lies:

I am responsible for what I see.
I choose the feelings I experience, and I decide upon the goal
I would achieve.
And everything that seems to happen to me I ask for, and
receive as I have asked.

Deceive yourself no longer that you are helpless in the face
of what is done to you. Acknowledge but that you have been
mistaken, and all effects of your mistakes will disappear.

It is impossible the Son of God be merely driven by events
outside of him. It is impossible that happenings that come to him
were not his choice. His power of decision is the determiner of every
situation in which he seems to find himself by chance or accident.[29]

Therefore, you do not have to change the outer world, but you do
have to change your own perception in order to experience the world
differently and to experience yourself differently. You can let go of
your nightmares of fear, sin, and guilt, and replace them with the
perception of the real world. The Course refers to the real world as
the "**happy dream**," because it is still a dream, but an illusion that
reflects the love of Heaven. To perceive your experience in the world
as a happy dream, you have the challenge of changing your thinking
from wrong-mindedness to **right-mindedness**.

Right-mindedness is not to be confused with the knowing
mind, because it is applicable only to right perception. You can be
right-minded or wrong-minded, and even this is subject to
degrees, clearly demonstrating that knowledge is not involved. The
term "right-mindedness" is properly used as the correction for
"wrong-mindedness," and applies to the state of mind that
induces accurate perception. It is miracle-minded because it heals
misperception, and this is indeed a miracle in view of how you
perceive yourself.[30]

Right-mindedness is brought about by listening to the Holy Spirit
instead of the ego. In your relationships, when a false perception is
exchanged for a true perception, a **miracle** occurs. Light and love
go to the receiver of the miracle and is returned equally to the giver
of the miracle. The miracle is an example of the Course principle that
"**giving and receiving are the same**."[31] The miracle always involves
an increase of light and love for the giver and receiver and requires no
loss or sacrifice at all.

False Forgiveness and True Forgiveness

~ ◦ ~

Right-mindedness brings about forgiveness, which is the primary tool used by the Holy Spirit to awaken the sleeping Sons of God. The purpose of forgiveness is to restore love by removing the obstacles to the awareness of love. Love is all that you really want because love is all that you really are, clearly stated this way: "...you *are* love. Love is your power, which the ego must deny."[32] According to the Course, you can do only two things: express love or call for love. But you mistakenly perceive your calls for love as sins rather than misguided seeking of love. You cannot return to your awareness of love as long as you are convinced by the ego that you are a guilty sinner. Because you feel guilty for your sins, you feel you must pay for what you have done. But God does not believe in karmic retribution, just as He does not believe in the reality of the dream world you have made.

There is cause and effect, but there is no karma as it is commonly understood in Eastern philosophy. Karma only seems to exist because of your illusory belief in the reality of guilt, which is a false and self-imposed belief in the necessity of self-punishment. When you experience what is generally called "karma," you are really just receiving the results of your past behavior that you have assigned to yourself based on what you feel you deserve. If you feel guilty, you will impose upon yourself some sort of self-punishment. In fact, this is the underlying cause of all sickness. Your guilt tells you that you deserve punishment and do not deserve love, but God knows that you deserve only love. God always loves you as His perfect Son. Since you are not guilty in God's eyes, you are not guilty at all—except in your own self-condemning eyes. To remove your sinful self-image requires only a change in thinking that will allow you to accept yourself as the innocent Son of God that you already are. Forgiveness enables you to make this change in thinking.

Because your belief in sin is entirely illusory and there is no karmic debt that needs to be paid, there is no need to seek forgiveness from an outside source. You receive the benefits of forgiveness by giving forgiveness to others.

Ask not to be forgiven, for this has already been accomplished. Ask, rather, to learn how to forgive, and to restore what always was to your unforgiving mind. Atonement becomes real and visible to those who use it. On earth this is your only function, and you must learn that it is all you want to learn. You will feel guilty till you learn this.[33]

Although you have no debt to pay for any of your sins, the Course does maintain that sins are merely "**mistakes**" or "**errors**" that can be corrected. The previous quote says you have already been forgiven, which means that all your mistakes have been corrected by the Holy Spirit. The term "Atonement" in the quote refers to the Holy Spirit's plan of salvation in which all errors and all their effects have been corrected. Thus the ego and its beliefs in sin and guilt have no power over you.

Forgiveness through the Holy Spirit lies simply in looking beyond error from the beginning, and thus keeping it unreal for you. Do not let any belief in its realness enter your mind, or you will also believe that you must undo what you have made in order to be forgiven. What has no effect does not exist, and to the Holy Spirit the effects of error are nonexistent. By steadily and consistently cancelling out all its effects, everywhere and in all respects, He teaches that the ego does not exist and proves it.[34]

Traditionally forgiveness automatically assumes that sin is real, the sinner should feel guilty, and punishment is justified. Having made these assumptions, forgiveness becomes a means of deceiving yourself about the truth. "You conceive of pardon as a vain attempt to look past what is there; to overlook the truth, in an unfounded effort to deceive yourself by making an illusion true."[35] As long as you think sin is real, you will believe that forgiveness must be a contradiction and a way of lying to yourself. "Because you think your sins are real, you look on pardon as deception. For it is impossible to think of sin as true and not believe forgiveness is a lie."[36] Forgiveness affirms the truth that others deserve to be pardoned. Yet it appears you must be lying to yourself when you forgive, because the belief in sin tells you that sinners are guilty and do not deserve to be pardoned. When sin is seen as real, this belief produces **false forgiveness**, which is given as an unwarranted gift to someone who is still seen as a guilty sinner. False forgiveness maintains the illusion that sin can take away your brother's holiness, which was given to him in his creation by God.

In stark contrast to false forgiveness, **true forgiveness** in the Course recognizes that guilt and sin are unreal. True forgiveness, which is based on right-mindedness, involves both "**looking and overlooking.**" The "overlooking" part of forgiveness looks past what is forgiven seeing that it is entirely an illusion that never happened in reality. Thus "overlooking" consists of "looking beyond error from the beginning, and thus keeping it unreal for you," as is quoted above. Yet keeping error unreal in your eyes can be tricky in your practical application of overlooking. "The ego's plan is to have you see error clearly first, and then overlook it. Yet how can you overlook what you have made real? By seeing it clearly, you have made it real and *cannot* overlook it."[37] Overlooking requires only that you recognize immediately at first glance that all fearful appearances of sin and guilt are illusory because they contradict the knowledge that every Son of God is just as holy now as when God created him in the eternal present moment. Therefore, it is necessary from the beginning to pay no attention to the details of what is forgiven as you practice overlooking.

The "looking" part of forgiveness sees only the divine holiness and true reality of the one who is forgiven, realizing he is always worthy of only love. Since he is worthy of love, you join with him. The ego is the idea of separation, which says there is a real gap of separation between you and your brother. However, when forgiveness occurs, you join with your brother, and you realize you are equals because he is just as holy as you are. "Forgiveness is the healing of the perception of separation."[38] Forgiveness then removes this illusory gap between you and your brother and proves to yourself that the ego, the whole idea of separation, is an illusion. What is this joining with your brother? Joining is the earthly version of love, which reflects the total joining that occurs in Heaven. You "can look with love or look with hate, depending only on the simple choice of whether you would join with what you see, or keep yourself apart and separate."[39] Forgiveness represents the choice to join. Thus forgiveness accomplishes your true goal of love, which is all that you really want.

Christ's Vision
Reveals the Real World

~ • ~

The Course is geared toward helping you to learn how to see the world, your brothers and sisters, and yourself differently. This requires a new and better vision than the form of seeing provided by your physical eyes. The "looking" for the divine, which is the joining part of forgiveness, is facilitated by **Christ's vision**, described in this way:

> Today we are trying to use a new kind of "projection." We are not attempting to get rid of what we do not like by seeing it outside. Instead, we are trying to see in the world what is in our minds, and what we want to recognize is there. Thus, we are trying to join with what we see, rather than keeping it apart from us. That is the fundamental difference between vision and the way you see.[40]

Projection is normally used in a misguided attempt to get rid of guilt in the mind by giving it to others. Representing the reversal of the projection of guilt, Christ's vision is a new form of projection in which light and love is seen in the others and in the world. Seeing the same light and love outwardly helps you to recognize that same light and love must be in your own mind. In this process of perceiving light and love outwardly and inwardly, you are joining with what you see, instead of producing the sense of separation that is the result of projecting guilt. This vision of light and love is a gift from Christ and the Holy Spirit that represents divine grace, requiring only your willingness to receive it.

> Christ's eyes are open, and He will look upon whatever you see with love if you accept His vision as yours. The Holy Spirit keeps the vision of Christ for every Son of God who sleeps. In His sight the Son of God is perfect, and He longs to share His vision with you. He will show you the real world because God gave you Heaven. Through Him your Father calls His Son to remember. The awakening of His Son begins with his investment in the real world, and by this he will learn to re-invest in himself. For reality is one with the Father and the Son, and the Holy Spirit blesses the real world in Their Name.[41]

Seeing not with the physical eyes, but with the "eyes of Christ" enables you to see the false as false and the true as true. Aided by the Holy Spirit, Christ's vision lets you see that illusions are unreal and that holiness is in every Son of God. Christ's vision leads to seeing the real world, which is the happy dream that contains only loving perceptions. The real world is itself an illusion because it is a world of perception, but it is the bridge that leads beyond perception back to Heaven.

> Salvation is nothing more than "right-mindedness," which is not the One-mindedness of the Holy Spirit, but which must be achieved before One-mindedness is restored. Right-mindedness leads to the next step automatically, because right perception is uniformly without attack, and therefore wrong-mindedness is obliterated. The ego cannot survive without judgment, and is laid aside accordingly. The mind then has only one direction in which it can move. Its direction is always automatic, because it cannot but be dictated by the thought system to which it adheres.[42]

The reason why the real world leads back to Heaven is that it is a forgiven world that has no judgments and no illusions of guilt in it. Thus the real world is not Heaven, but it is a reflection of Heaven. The loving perceptions of the real world are so much like the love in Heaven that the transfer from the partial awareness of perceptions to the total awareness of knowledge in Heaven becomes possible and even inevitable. However, if you exclude anyone from your loving forgiveness, you will bar the door to Heaven for yourself. To open the door to Heaven, you must generalize your learning to apply forgiveness and Christ's vision of holiness to every situation and to every person without exception. Thus you come Home by becoming a savior for your brothers and sisters, even as you will see them becoming saviors for you.

> For the Holy Spirit will lead everyone home to his Father, where Christ waits as his Self.
> Every child of God is one in Christ, for his being is in Christ as Christ's is in God. Christ's Love for you is His Love for His Father, which He knows because He knows His Father's Love for Him. When the Holy Spirit has at last led you to Christ at the altar to His Father, perception fuses into knowledge because perception has become so holy that its transfer to holiness is merely its natural extension. Love transfers to love without any interference, for the two are one. As you perceive more and more

common elements in all situations, the transfer of training under the Holy Spirit's guidance increases and becomes generalized. Gradually you learn to apply it to everyone and everything, for its applicability is universal. When this has been accomplished, perception and knowledge have become so similar that they share the unification of the laws of God.

What is one cannot be perceived as separate, and the denial of the separation is the reinstatement of knowledge. At the altar of God, the holy perception of God's Son becomes so enlightened that light streams into it, and the spirit of God's Son shines in the Mind of the Father and becomes one with it. Very gently does God shine upon Himself, loving the extension of Himself that is His Son. The world has no purpose as it blends into the purpose of God. For the real world has slipped quietly into Heaven, where everything eternal in it has always been. There the Redeemer and the redeemed join in perfect love of God and of each other. Heaven is your home, and being in God it must also be in you. [43]

The Holy Relationship
and Jesus

~ • ~

One of the best means that the Holy Spirit uses to teach forgiveness that leads to awakening is the **holy relationship**. Whenever two people join for a common purpose with common interests, they form a holy relationship. The common purpose can be a lofty one or even a mundane one. For example, two partners can come together to accomplish the common purpose of writing a book on healthy eating. But they must have common interests in the pursuit of that common purpose. One partner may be motivated to write the book in order to make money for himself. The other partner may be motivated to write the book to help others live a healthier life. Since one has a selfish interest motivating him and the other has an unselfish interest, they do not have common interests, and so this would not be in a holy relationship. On the other hand, if both partners have the same unselfish interests, they would be united in a holy relationship. Holy relationship partners join for what they can gain together rather than for what they can gain separately.

The time of joining in the holy relationship is an example of a **holy instant**, a time in which normal habits of thinking and feeling are set aside. During this pause in normal functioning, there is an openness to receiving the divine truth that reflects Heaven. In the holy instant of joining, the Holy Spirit enters the holy relationship, and He leads you together in your common purpose. Although you may start out having only a mundane common purpose, the Holy Spirit will help you to eventually accept His higher purpose of holiness.

In fact, the Course itself came into being as the direct result of a holy relationship that was formed in 1965 between Bill Thetford, 42, and Helen Schucman, 56. Bill considered himself an agnostic, and Helen claimed to be an atheist, making them unlikely candidates to bring forth the Course. They were both employed as professors in a medical psychology department associated with Columbia University. Being discouraged by all the problems in their psychology department, Bill told Helen he was determined to find a "better way" of dealing with their problems. Helen decided to join with him in the common purpose of finding a better way. That was their holy instant of joining in which the

Holy Spirit entered the relationship. Subsequently, Helen began to hear an inner Voice speak to her. The voice said, "This is a course in miracles. Please take notes." She told Bill about the Voice and that she was afraid she was going insane. Bill calmly suggested that she write down what the Voice said, and he offered to get together with her to discern whether or not the Voice made any sense. Helen reluctantly agreed with Bill's suggestion, and she became the "scribe" for the following words that now serve as the introduction to the Course:

> *This is a course in miracles. It is a required course. Only the time you take it is voluntary. Free will does not mean that you can establish the curriculum. It means only that you can elect what you want to take at a given time. The course does not aim at teaching the meaning of love, for that is beyond what can be taught. It does aim, however, at removing the blocks to the awareness of love's presence, which is your natural inheritance. The opposite of love is fear, but what is all-encompassing can have no opposite.*

> *This course can therefore be summed up very simply in this way:*

> **Nothing real can be threatened.**
> **Nothing unreal exists.**

> *Herein lies the peace of God.*[44]

After seven years of Helen taking notes and their processing of the information, the result was *A Course in Miracles*. When Bill and Helen came together to form their holy relationship, they had no idea that their joining for the purpose of seeking a better way in their psychology department would provide a means of finding a better way for many seekers throughout the world. The Holy Spirit had a plan for their lives greater than they could possibly have imagined. Perhaps the inspirational story of Helen and Bill will help you to recognize that the Holy Spirit has a plan for your life that is similarly greater than you can imagine.

Helen did not seek the spotlight, and she wanted to be known only as the "scribe" of the Course because she definitely did not want anyone to think of her as its author. The Voice dictating to Helen spoke in such a way as to clearly indicate that Jesus was the actual author of the Course in coordination with the Holy Spirit. Here is what the Course says about Jesus:

He has become the risen Son of God. He has overcome death because he has accepted life. He has recognized himself as God created him, and in so doing he has recognized all living things as part of him. There is now no limit on his power, because it is the power of God. So has his name become the Name of God, for he no longer sees himself as separate from Him.[45]

According to the Course, Jesus is your awakened brother and your equal in Christ. Therefore, Jesus is not more loved by God than you are loved by God. In the first chapter of the Course, Jesus describes his role in relationship to you in this way:

> You stand below me and I stand below God. In the process of "rising up," I am higher because without me the distance between God and man would be too great for you to encompass. I bridge the distance as an elder brother to you on the one hand, and as a Son of God on the other. My devotion to my brothers has placed me in charge of the Sonship, which I render complete because I share it. [46]

The goal of Jesus, in coordination with the Holy Spirit, is to help you become what he is now by assisting you to wake up from your dreams of separation. He encourages you to join with your brothers and sisters to form holy relationships, as Helen Schucman and Bill Thetford joined in a common purpose. The holy relationship is one of the primary means of learning the lessons of forgiveness that lead to the real world and that facilitate waking up. The holy relationship heals the separation that appears to exist between you and your brother and that keeps you from awakening. "Forget not that a shadow held between your brother and yourself obscures the face of Christ and memory of God."[47] Through the holy relationship, you forgive your brother, and you see no separation, no sin, no guilt between you and your partner that would obscure your vision of the face of Christ.

> When brothers join in purpose in the world of fear, they stand already at the edge of the real world. Perhaps they still look back, and think they see an idol that they want. Yet has their path been surely set away from idols toward reality. For when they joined their hands it was Christ's hand they took, and they will look on Him Whose hand they hold. The face of Christ is looked upon before the Father is remembered. For He must be unremembered till His Son has reached beyond forgiveness to the Love of God. Yet is the Love of Christ accepted first. And then will come the knowledge They are One.[48]

Visions are always symbolic and are within the realm of perception. Therefore, the face of Christ, which is a vision, is a symbolic image of Christ, but is not Christ Himself, Who resides in the knowledge of Heaven and beyond perception. Yet the image of the face of Christ is the loftiest vision, the most pure image at the deepest level of the real world. It is the most perfect reflection of Christ and of Heaven that can be seen in a vision. For that reason this perfect vision of the face of Christ enkindles the memory of God. In the separation you gave yourself "the great amnesia in which the memory of God seems quite forgotten."[49] But seeing the face of Christ offers the opportunity to remember your Father. After you have directly seen the face of Christ and regained the memory of your Father, then God Himself takes the final step of lifting you back to your true Home in Heaven.

> Yet even forgiveness is not the end. Forgiveness does make lovely, but it does not create. It is the source of healing, but it is the messenger of love and not its Source. Here you are led, that God Himself can take the final step unhindered, for here does nothing interfere with love, letting it be itself. A step beyond this holy place of forgiveness, a step still further inward but the one *you* cannot take, transports you to something completely different. Here is the Source of light; nothing perceived, forgiven nor transformed. But merely known.[50]

The Holy Spirit's plan of Atonement is not just for some selected individuals who make their way to Heaven through learning how to forgive, reaching the real world, and seeing the face of Christ. It is everyone's destiny. "The real world is the symbol that the dream of sin and guilt is over, and God's Son no longer sleeps. His waking eyes perceive the sure reflection of his Father's Love; the certain promise that he is redeemed."[51] The lessons of forgiveness leading to the real world restore every seeker's true Identity when God takes His final step. "And as we look upon a world forgiven, it is He [God Himself] Who calls to us and comes to take us home, reminding us of our Identity which our forgiveness has restored to us."[52]

The Role of Meditation

~ ₒ ~

Many Eastern philosophies recognize that the world is an illusion and advocate the inward-seeking practices of meditation as the means of awakening from this illusion. The Course maintains the following:

> It is extremely difficult to reach Atonement [salvation from your errors] by fighting against sin. Enormous effort is expended in the attempt to make holy what is hated and despised. Nor is a lifetime of contemplation and long periods of meditation aimed at detachment from the body necessary. All such attempts will ultimately succeed because of their purpose. Yet the means are tedious and very time consuming, for all of them look to the future for release from a state of present unworthiness and inadequacy.[53]

This quotation comes from a section titled, "I need do nothing," and it is misunderstood by some Course students because they assume it means that any form of meditation is not helpful. Yet it is only referring to forms of meditation that affirm sinfulness rather than holiness. The Manual for Teacher's part of the Course advises having a quiet time of inward attunement devoted to God every morning and evening. Yet no one specific meditation method is recommended for these daily quiet times. It is also clear that the Workbook part of the Course offers a variety of techniques that lead in the direction of experiencing the divine presence. "I need do nothing" refers to meditation that helps you find a place of rest within.

> To do nothing is to rest, and make a place within you where the activity of the body ceases to demand attention. Into this place the Holy Spirit comes, and there abides. He will remain when you forget, and the body's activities return to occupy your conscious mind.[54]

The Course sometimes suggests some visual imagery as part of inward seeking. Furthermore, a few Workbook lessons recommend repeating the Name of God for meditation. The Name of Jesus can be used as a symbol for the Name of God. The following quotation explains the significance of the Name of Jesus:

The name of Jesus Christ as such is but a symbol. But it stands for love that is not of this world. It is a symbol that is safely used as a replacement for the many names of all the gods to which you pray. It becomes the shining symbol for the Word of God, so close to what it stands for that the little space between the two is lost, the moment that the name is called to mind. Remembering the name of Jesus Christ is to give thanks for all the gifts that God has given you. [55]

Other than the continuous repetition of the Name of God, repeating words throughout the entire meditation is not recommended. The attunement method most recommended is repeating a few sacred words to counteract mental distractions. After your mind becomes calm through temporarily repeating these inspiring words, you can let go of all words to feel the divine presence within. If your mind becomes distracted again, you can briefly go back to repeating the inspiring words. Generally speaking, the Course seems to be saying that any technique will be sufficient as long as it does not reinforce your sense of sinfulness in an attempt to reach God while at the same time feeling you are unworthy of Him. Any approach that accepts the belief in your sinfulness is not effective because it is an attempt to make yourself holy while thinking you are basically unholy.

You make it difficult for yourself if you are seeking God while also believing you are unworthy of Him. Your ego volunteers to help you seek God. Nevertheless, the ego uses the ideas of fear, sin, and guilt to ensure that God and His Love cannot be found. This is the reason why meditation is only a complimentary means of spiritual growth and is not the primary means of awakening in the Course. Forgiveness is regarded in the Course as a much better tool for awakening because it directly overcomes the major obstacle to awakening, which is the mistaken belief that sin and guilt are real.

Nevertheless, meditation and forgiveness are approaches to spiritual growth that have two common elements. The first common element is related to the interpersonal nature of both. Obviously forgiveness is an extension of love in which you join with another person and see your equality and oneness with him. Meditation may appear to be a solitary activity, yet you meditate to experience divine love within. Thus you are seeking union with God *and* with in the Sonship. In successful meditation you experience your oneness with God and your brothers and sisters in the Sonship, similar to the extension of love that occurs in forgiveness. The other element that meditation and forgiveness have in common is explained at the end of the next section.

The Three Stages of
Learning Forgiveness

~ ⚬ ~

You may wonder why forgiveness is so important and why love is not considered the best tool for the transformation of consciousness. After all, love is what everyone wants. The greatest obstacle to transforming consciousness is your ego. When you seek to apply love toward your spiritual growth, the ego is undeterred because it can quite easily manipulate your attempts at love. In fact, the ego quickly volunteers to be your guide to seeking love. The ego's secret motto is "seek but do not find."[56] The ego can afford to promise you love because it can so effectively ensure your failure. The tools used by the ego to undermine love are the beliefs in separation, sin, and guilt, which all induce fear and prevent love.

Before love can truly be found, the ego's instruments of separation, sin, and guilt must be disabled. Forgiveness is your means of removing these obstacles to love. That's why the Course's introduction quoted on page 31 states that the aim of learning is "*removing the blocks to the awareness of love's presence.*" Forgiveness helps you overcome the vice grip the ego has on your mind. Forgiveness possesses the one thing the ego can never have: the truth. The truth that forgiveness presents is simply that illusions have no power over you and that your true holiness is your salvation. Forgiveness disempowers your beliefs in separation, sin, and guilt by recognizing they are not real. With these obstacles unmasked as illusions and removed, forgiveness reminds you of your holiness and restores the awareness of love. Your growth in learning forgiveness has three stages.

STAGE ONE OF LEARNING FORGIVENESS

Stage One is *motivation and understanding.* Your starting point for learning forgiveness is your **motivation** for wanting to make a change in your life. That motivation is **pain**. Think of the example previously given of Helen Schucman and Bill Thetford. They recognized the painful situation in their work environment, and in their response to that pain, they sought a better way. The Course maintains that everyone will eventually seek a better way.

The acceptance of the Atonement by everyone is only a matter of time. This may appear to contradict free will because of the inevitability of the final decision, but this is not so. You can temporize and you are capable of enormous procrastination, but you cannot depart entirely from your Creator, Who set the limits on your ability to miscreate. An imprisoned will engenders a situation which, in the extreme, becomes altogether intolerable. Tolerance for pain may be high, but it is not without limit. Eventually everyone begins to recognize, however dimly, that there *must* be a better way. As this recognition becomes more firmly established, it becomes a turning point.[57]

Remember the Atonement is the Holy Spirit's plan that will return everyone to Heaven, and everyone must accept their role in this plan. It's not enough to just feel pain and want a better way. You must also choose a way that really is better than the one the ego shows you that causes your pain. For example, a person may want to reduce pain in his life and may think jumping off a cliff to end it all would be a better way. But according to the Course, suicide does not produce a real change that would heal the split mind. Consequently, along with the motivation to move in a new and better direction, you must also have the proper **understanding** of what that better way is.

Perhaps the pain in your life will motivate you to study the Course to gain the understanding that would actually show you a better way. This first stage of forgiveness is directly related to the Course's Text, which provides the intellectual understanding of the spiritual principles that form the basis for finding a better way. You can read the Text once, but you may still not understand the implications of its concepts.

Once you have developed a thought system of any kind, you live by it and teach it. Your capacity for allegiance to a thought system may be misplaced, but it is still a form of faith and can be redirected.[58]

You already have a thought system in place. You have put your faith in it. Are you willing to redirect your beliefs and faith toward the radically different thought system that is offered to you in the Text? For example, are you willing to replace the ideas of sin and guilt in your current thought system with the new definitions of these ideas in the Course? Are you willing to accept the Course's description of forgiveness, which perceives sin and guilt as unreal in your brother and in yourself and perceives holiness as real in your brother and in yourself? Let's assume that you intellectually comprehend the new

Course ideas of forgiveness and that you are at least willing to see for yourself if these new ideas are in fact true as they relate to your life and relationships.

STAGE TWO OF LEARNING FORGIVENESS

Stage Two is *application and healing*. Your understanding gained through studying the Text will be just another theory to you until you put that understanding into practical **application**. Here is where the Course's Workbook for Students comes in. Its 365 daily lessons give you a full year to train your mind to perceive everyone and everything in the world differently through the eyes of forgiveness.

In the first stage you gain an understanding of the theoretical side of the Course's spiritual principles, but your comprehension does not necessarily mean that you would believe in the truth and usefulness of those principles. The Workbook reassures you that you do not need to believe the ideas in order to use them.

> Some of the ideas the workbook presents you will find hard to believe, and others may seem to be quite startling. This does not matter. You are merely asked to apply the ideas as you are directed to do. You are not asked to judge them at all. You are asked only to use them. It is their use that will give them meaning to you, and will show you that they are true.[59]

As was described previously, forgiveness is a two-part process that includes "overlooking" and then "looking." Therefore, the Workbook is divided into two sections. The first section deals with training your mind to let go of the way you currently perceive the world. This section provides lessons in applying the "overlooking" part of forgiveness, which is the undoing of the false perceptions of sin and guilt you have projected upon others and the world. The second section of the Workbook is about acquiring true perception. This section offers lessons in applying the "looking" part of forgiveness, which uses true perception to see the divine in others and in the world. In your practice of "looking" what do you focus on to see the divine with forgiving eyes? You can focus on seeing holiness, light, love, goodness, or peace in others. You can focus on seeing God, Christ, or the Holy Spirit in others. You choose whatever offers you the best window to seeing the divine in others.

The application of forgiveness brings about the healing of the split mind. Many problems seem to be in the world, but the Course asserts there is really only one problem. This one problem is the split mind, which needs to be healed and is healed as the result of forgiveness.

Your split mind does not separate you from God, but does conceal your awareness of God. Forgiveness guided by the Holy Spirit does not focus directly on forgiving yourself for your split mind. Instead, it focuses on releasing fear. Before the separation you had an "intense and burning love of God,"[60] which is even now hidden in your split mind. As a result of the separation, you acquired your first and greatest fear, which is your fear of God that was the result of the separation. If you consider that God is Love, then your fear of God at its deepest level is really a fear of love. From this perspective you are actually afraid of redemption because salvation will bring God's Love and with it complete union with Him. This will demolish your entire sense of separation, which your ego clings to tenaciously.

> You have built your whole insane belief system because you think you would be helpless in God's Presence, and you would save yourself from His Love because you think it would crush you into nothingness. You are afraid it would sweep you away from yourself and make you little, because you believe that magnitude lies in defiance, and that attack is grandeur. You think you have made a world God would destroy; and by loving Him, which you do, you would throw this world away, which you *would*. Therefore, you have used the world to cover your love, and the deeper you go into the blackness of the ego's foundation, the closer you come to the Love that is hidden there. *And it is this that frightens you.*[61]

Indeed, God would give you salvation right now if you were not so afraid of it. Mixed in with your fear of redemption is a certain amount of pride because: "You can accept insanity because you made it, but you cannot accept love because you did not."[62] Pride's opposite partner, which is self-condemnation, plays a much larger role as it brings its dark and stinging influence either consciously or subconsciously. Every minute of every day you are choosing either fear or love and either illusion or the truth. The wrong-mindedness of self-condemnation overlooks the loving sights that the right-mindedness of forgiveness would look for. Likewise, self-condemnation looks for the fearful illusions that forgiveness would overlook. The ego offers to be your "friend" to protect you from the fear of God and fear of His Love. The ego provides the fuel for delaying your acceptance of redemption by supplying you with the fearful beliefs in your guilt and sinfulness that tell you of your unworthiness of God's Love. You cling to these "gifts" of the ego because you think salvation rests in illusions rather than in the reality of God's unfailing and eternal Love with which He created you, giving you His Holiness.

Yet if you could remember your holiness given to you by God, you would realize that you are not guilty and you are worthy of God's Love. Thus you have no need to fear God. But right now God is very abstract to you because your current awareness with your split mind is concrete. You can find your holiness again and heal your fear of God through healing your concrete relationships with your brothers and sisters, who are Sons of God, just as you are. It is your "holiness that points to God," and it is your "holiness that makes you safe. It is denied if you attack any brother for anything. For it is here the split with God occurs."[63]

Just as you loved God before the separation, you loved all the other Sons of God. You gave yourself to all of the Sonship in a joyous and loving expansion of yourself. Just as you became afraid of God after the separation, you became afraid of your brothers. You contracted into your private and very limited world of the ego based on fear and isolation. Seeing guilt within, you denied it and projected it outward onto your brothers. Your split mind needs healing that only forgiveness can provide. By seeing your brother through the loving eyes of forgiveness, you withdraw your judgments and projections you had laid upon your brother. Instead of separating from your brother, you join with him and see yourself in him. Seeing holiness in him convinces you that holiness must be in you as well. Your brother accepts your loving forgiveness and changes his image of himself, believing he is worthy of the love that is given. In gratitude, your brother returns the love that he receives from your forgiveness. This loving mutual exchange is a miracle, which brings healing to both the mind of the giver and receiver of forgiveness.

Your application of forgiveness shows that you have decided to abandon the ego as your guide and have accepted the Holy Spirit as your guide. When you practice forgiveness, the healing that results is not accomplished *by* you; it is accomplished *through* you. The Holy Spirit is the facilitator of healing for both your mind and the person who is forgiven by you.

Perhaps you see how forgiveness can heal a relationship here and there, but how can forgiveness entirely heal the split mind by producing an entire transformation of consciousness, not only for you, but for the world? For the answer, let's look at the next stage of learning forgiveness.

STAGE THREE OF LEARNING FORGIVENESS

Stage Three is *teaching and generalization*. The second stage of forgiveness gets you in touch with the application of forgiveness, which results in healing. The third stage is a deepening of your experience of applying forgiveness. This more intense and consistent experience of forgiveness is the result of **teaching** what you have learned. Studying the Course's Manual for Teachers helps you to grow in the direction of becoming a teacher of God. You don't have to be a formal teacher with students in order to teach. In fact, you simply teach by your example, which shows that you believe in the thought system ruled by the ego or the thought system inspired by the Holy Spirit. You teach what you want to learn, and you learn by teaching, which is a gift you give to yourself. When you choose the Holy Spirit as your guide, your teaching is your demonstration of your belief in guiltlessness and forgiveness.

> A teacher of God is anyone who chooses to be one. His qualifications consist solely in this; somehow, somewhere he has made a deliberate choice in which he did not see his interests as apart from someone else's.[64]

The teachers of God who teach the Course teach "a special curriculum, intended for teachers of a special form of the universal course."[65] In other words, the Course is one of "many thousands of other forms, all with the same outcome."[66] The forms of the universal Course vary, but their content always has the same theme, which is: "God's Son is guiltless, and in his innocence is his salvation."[67]

To be a teacher of God who teaches the special curriculum of the Course requires that you study all of the Text, complete the entire year of daily Workbook lessons, and read the Manual. Then the teacher must demonstrate what he has learned by how he lives his life. The teacher of God understands the importance of the **generalization** of learning, which is the hallmark of the third stage of learning forgiveness. The idea of generalization is emphasized in the introduction to the Workbook. The lessons are designed to "help you to generalize the ideas involved to every situation in which you find yourself, and to everyone and everything in it."[68] In the typical learning of the world, for example, you study geology and math as totally separate experiences. But in the learning promoted in the Course, you are retraining your perception to see how all things are interrelated and eventually to see that everything is joined in oneness.

In the second stage of forgiveness, it appears that forgiveness can heal some relationships in your life. However, in this third stage with more experience at manifesting forgiveness, you gain a greater appreciation for the generalization of forgiveness. You can clearly see that forgiveness stretches far beyond letting go of specific grievances between you and others. You can better understand how forgiveness produces an entire transformation of consciousness, not only for healing your split mind, but for healing others and even the world.

The unforgiving mind engaged in normal perception sees a world in which every person and object is separate from everything else. The forgiving mind sees in the real world, in the happy dream, the underlying unity and divine presence in every person and every object. But the forgiving mind must itself be unified with all true perceptions. Even one unloving false perception will negate the unity of the mind and will prevent seeing the real world that contains only loving true perceptions.

Transfer of training in true perception does not proceed as does transfer of the training of the world. If true perception has been achieved in connection with any person, situation or event, total transfer to everyone and everything is certain. On the other hand, one exception held apart from true perception makes its accomplishments anywhere impossible.[69]

In this world of form everyone appears to have a private mind encased in a separate body. But the mind is not contained by the body and is not private. In fact, all minds are joined now, in spite of the appearance to the contrary. This means that what happens in one mind affects all minds. Every uplifting thought of forgiveness reverberates throughout all of the Sonship. The Holy Spirit plays the central role in generalizing your learning of forgiveness and brings the benefits of healing to all minds, since the Holy Spirit is in all minds and reminds them of their unity.

The Holy Spirit will eventually help you to generalize your learning of forgiveness to such a degree that you will use Christ's vision everywhere to see everyone. Then you will see the real world of only loving thoughts of forgiveness. The unreal world of dark dreams will turn into the happy dream, which is still an illusion, yet it becomes a doorway to Heaven.

The unreal world *is* a thing of despair, for it can never be. And you who share God's Being with Him could never be content without reality. What God did not give you has no power over you, and the attraction of love for love remains irresistible. For it is the function of love to unite all things unto itself, and to hold all things together by extending its wholeness.

The real world was given you by God in loving exchange for the world you made and the world you see. Only take it from the hand of Christ and look upon it. Its reality will make everything else invisible, for beholding it is total perception. And as you look upon it you will remember that it was always so. Nothingness will become invisible, for you will at last have seen truly. Redeemed perception is easily translated into knowledge, for only perception is capable of error and perception has never been. Being corrected it gives place to knowledge, which is forever the only reality. The Atonement is but the way back to what was never lost. Your Father could not cease to love His Son.[70]

When you generalize your learning in the Course, you see how all your various spiritual practices are interrelated as they lead you toward oneness. This section has described the stages of learning forgiveness and a previous section addressed the role of meditation in the Course. Obviously both forgiveness and meditation have the same purpose of helping you make progress toward the single ultimate goal of spiritual awakening. It may seem equally obvious that they are very different means of growing spiritually. What may not be so obvious is that the apparently different approaches are not really so different after all. The book *Christian Meditation Inspired by Yoga and "A Course in Miracles"* explains how forgiveness and meditation are totally interrelated. The following excerpt from this book summarizes their interrelationship:

Thus both forgiveness and meditation help you grow toward the common goal of oneness, but are they really distinctly different ways of seeking oneness? No, they seek oneness in the same way. *Forgiveness is meditation applied outwardly toward others.* Meditation is the mental holding of one thought of the divine in the mind and the letting go all other distracting thoughts. In practicing forgiveness, just as in practicing meditation, you are letting go of distracting thoughts by overlooking all your judgments against the person you are forgiving. Likewise, you are holding the one thought of looking for the divine in the person you are forgiving, similar to the way you hold on to the one thought of seeing the divine within yourself in practicing meditation.

Forgiveness and meditation have a reciprocal relationship. Since forgiveness is meditation applied outwardly, the inverse is equally true: *Meditation is forgiveness applied inwardly toward yourself.* When you forgive your brother by letting go of your grievances, you are helping your brother to heal his mind and simultaneously helping to heal your own mind. Your forgiveness of others is really a means of forgiving yourself. Yet this process of forgiving yourself can also be done directly by the inner practices of meditation. After all, when you go within you are letting go of distracting thoughts and judgments. You are attempting to go past these distractions, which are inner grievances that you are holding against yourself. These grievances hide your true nature. Just as you can see the divine in your brother by letting go of grievances, you can apply forgiveness toward yourself by looking past your inner grievances to find the divine within.

Accepting the Atonement

~ ● ~

The way back to God is the Atonement, His plan of return. The only function of the teacher of God is to forgive by accepting the Atonement Likewise, the only responsibility of the miracle worker is to forgive by accepting the Atonement for himself. Acceptance of the Atonement is the acceptance of perfect love that corrects all errors and ends all illusions of separation. By accepting the Atonement, the mind of the healer is healed in the holy instant, and then in that same holy instant healing happens to others not *by* him, but *through* him by the action of the Holy Spirit.

In order to heal, it thus becomes essential for the teacher of God to let all his own mistakes be corrected. If he senses even the faintest hint of irritation in himself as he responds to anyone, let him instantly realize that he has made an interpretation that is not true. Then let him turn within to his eternal Guide, and let Him judge what the response should be. So is he healed, and in his healing is his pupil healed with him. The sole responsibility of God's teacher is to accept the Atonement for himself. Atonement means correction, or the undoing of errors. When this has been accomplished, the teacher of God becomes a miracle worker by definition. His sins have been forgiven him, and he no longer condemns himself. How can he then condemn anyone? And who is there whom his forgiveness can fail to heal?[71]

The Atonement must eventually be accepted by everyone since it is the Holy Spirit's plan of salvation for all the sleeping Sons of God. There is a lower level of accepting the Atonement and an ultimate level of accepting the Atonement. Likewise, there is a lower level of seeing the face of Christ and an ultimate level of seeing the face of Christ. These lower levels of accepting that Atonement and seeing the face of Christ involve specific individual instances of forgiveness. "That forgiveness is healing needs to be understood, if the teacher of God is to make progress."[72] Here is an example of the healing provided by the teacher of God:

He overlooks the mind *and* body, seeing only the face of Christ shining in front of him, correcting all mistakes and healing all perception. Healing is the result of the recognition, by God's teacher, of who it is that is in need of healing. This recognition has no special reference. It is true of all things that God created. In it are all illusions healed.

When a teacher of God fails to heal, it is because he has forgotten Who he is. Another's sickness thus becomes his own. In allowing this to happen, he has identified with another's ego, and has thus confused him with a body. In so doing, he has refused to accept the Atonement for himself, and can hardly offer it to his brother in Christ's Name. He will, in fact, be unable to recognize his brother at all, for his Father did not create bodies, and so he is seeing in his brother only the unreal. Mistakes do not correct mistakes, and distorted perception does not heal. Step back now, teacher of God. You have been wrong. Lead not the way, for you have lost it. Turn quickly to your Teacher, and let yourself be healed.

The offer of Atonement is universal. It is equally applicable to all individuals in all circumstances.[73]

In particular occurrences of healing, the teacher of God sees the face of Christ in the one receiving the healing, and the teacher of God accepts the Atonement for himself to facilitate the healing. The challenge presented to the teacher of God is to generalize his learning so he does not limit its application, yet it may take him a long time to learn this lesson,

> The progress of the teacher of God may be slow or rapid, depending on whether he recognizes the Atonement's inclusiveness, or for a time excludes some problem areas from it. In some cases, there is a sudden and complete awareness of the perfect applicability of the lesson of the Atonement to all situations, but this is comparatively rare. The teacher of God may have accepted the function God has given him long before he has learned all that his acceptance holds out to him. It is only the end that is certain. Anywhere along the way, the necessary realization of inclusiveness may reach him.[74]

If the teacher of God manages to finally generalize his learning, he will perceive the face of Christ in everyone and everything without exception. He will also consistently accept the Atonement and apply forgiveness to every situation, without missing any opportunity to extend healing through the action of the Holy Spirit. Then in this total generalization, the teacher of God eventually will see the ultimate face of Christ and fully accept the Atonement at the deepest level of the real world. Here the face of Christ is the ultimate vision of awakening that brings back the memory of God. Here Atonement is the inner content of that ultimate vision—the content of perfect love. At this time God takes the final step of bringing about the teacher of God's awakening and return to Heaven. God gives his final judgment of the Son of God, which is:

> *Holy are you, eternal, free and whole, at peace forever in the Heart of God. Where is the world, and where is sorrow now?*

Is this your judgment on yourself, teacher of God? Do you believe that this is wholly true? No; not yet, not yet. But this is still your goal; why you are here. It is your function to prepare yourself to hear this Judgment and to recognize that it is true. One instant of complete belief in this, and you will go beyond belief to Certainty. One instant out of time can bring time's end.[75]

Before this final judgment can occur, the teacher of God will need to let go of his deepest and last fear, which is the fear of God. It is the destiny of the teacher of God and indeed all seekers to eventually overcome this final fear and hear God proclaim the sinlessness of His Son. "But the Final Judgment will not come until it is no longer associated with fear. One day each one will welcome it, and on that very day it will be given him."[76] Fortunately the full acceptance of the Atonement that has brought him to the deepest level of the real world will also relieve him of his fear of God. The Atonement accomplishes this because "Fear arises from lack of love. The only remedy for lack of love is perfect love. Perfect love is the Atonement."[77] The teacher of God does not make this happen, but merely accepts that this has already happened by the action of the Holy Spirit, Who is the Mind of the Atonement.

The Function of Healing

≈ ◦ ≈

There is definitely an overlapping of meaning in many concepts found in the Course. For instance, the face of Christ and the Atonement can be thought of as two sides of the same coin in regard to issues such as healing and bringing the teacher of God to his final awakening. Another example of this kind of overlapping and close relationship of ideas is Christ's vision and forgiveness. Christ's vision is what makes miracles of healing possible. Forgiveness is the content of that vision similarly making miracles of healing possible. Therefore, Christ's vision and forgiveness are not distinctly separate ideas. In fact, all the basic spiritual concepts are presented in ways that highlight how they interrelate rather than how they are distinctly different and separate. Through teaching you that spiritual ideas are interrelated and are not separate, the Course is showing you that you are defined by your own interrelationships with all the other Sons of God, with the Holy Spirit, and with God Himself. The Course even says directly that you are an *idea* in the Mind of God and that is why you can give all of yourself in loving extension to all parts of the Sonship without losing, but only gaining love. After all, when you share an idea even in this world, you are able to keep the idea even while you give it away to another person.

Although it is clear that the apparently different concepts in the Course are actually interrelated and in many ways overlap each other, what may not be clear yet is how all of these concepts are moving in the same direction. When you use Christ's vision, you will learn to understand, appreciate, and apply the lessons of oneness presented to you by the Holy Spirit. The significance of increasing your awareness and application of oneness is summarized in the following way:

Seeing with Him will show you that all meaning, including yours, comes not from double vision, but from the gentle fusing of everything into *one* meaning, *one* emotion and *one* purpose. God has one purpose which He shares with you. The single vision which the Holy Spirit offers you will bring this oneness to your mind with clarity and brightness so intense you could not wish, for all the world, not to accept what God would have you have. Behold your will, accepting it as His, with all His Love as yours.[78]

What is this one purpose that God shares with you? God's Will for you, as well as your own true will, is to wake up in Heaven. Thus this one purpose is **awakening**. In order to accomplish your one purpose of waking up in Heaven, you will need to accept your one function, which is **healing**. Twelve basic concepts of the Course are listed below along with Course quotations. Notice how all of these Course concepts are related to moving in the direction of healing:

TEACHER OF GOD — Whenever a teacher of God has tried to be a channel for healing he has succeeded.[79]

THE FACE OF CHRIST — The holy instant's radiance will light your eyes, and give them sight to see beyond all suffering and see Christ's face instead. Healing replaces suffering.[80]

THE LOVE OF CHRIST — Answer his call for love, and yours is answered. Healing is the Love of Christ for His Father and for Himself.[81]

THE ATONEMENT — Healing and Atonement are not related; they are identical.[82]

CHRIST'S VISION — Everyone seen without the past thus brings you nearer to the end of time by bringing healed and healing sight into the darkness, and enabling the world to see. For light must come into the darkened world to make Christ's vision possible even here.[83]

THE REAL WORLD — Just as forgiveness overlooks all sins that never were accomplished, healing but removes illusions that have not occurred. Just as the real world will arise to take the place of what has never been at all, healing but offers restitution for imagined states and false ideas which dreams embroider into pictures of the truth.[84]

A MIRACLE — A miracle of healing proves that separation is without effect.[85]

THE HOLY INSTANT — Come to the holy instant and be healed, for nothing that is there received is left behind on your returning to the world.[86]

THE HOLY RELATIONSHIP — This holy relationship has the power to heal all pain, regardless of its form.[87]

THE HOLY SPIRIT — The Holy Spirit promotes healing by looking beyond it to what the children of God were before healing was needed, and will be when they have been healed.[88]

RIGHT-MINDEDNESS — If you do accept it, you are in a position to recognize that those who need healing are simply those who have not realized that right-mindedness *is* healing.[89]

FORGIVENESS — Forgiveness is not real unless it brings a healing to your brother and yourself.[90]

The quotations above show that the Course itself is a unified thought system. Its apparently different concepts are not really so different. These concepts are interconnected by their single unified purpose of spiritual awakening, which in turn is centered upon the one means of achieving that purpose—your function of healing.

Unification of the Mind

~ ๐ ~

If healing is your function, what is it that needs to be healed? As was stated previously, the mind that perceives is a split mind and must be healed to wake up in Heaven. Healing the body is only a secondary objective of healing because all sickness of the body is the result of an unhealed mind. Your purpose, which is also God's purpose, is for your mind to return to the One-mindedness of Heaven, which is another term for the total awareness of knowledge. However, you cannot wake to One-mindedness until your split mind is healed. With your current split mind, you carry an endless number of separate perceptions in your mind. But to heal your split mind, you will have to eventually unify your thought system, following the same pattern established by the Course. In other words, you must set clearly in your mind your purpose of spiritual awakening and likewise establish your means of awakening as healing primarily through forgiveness, because: "To forgive is to heal."[91]

In order to facilitate the unification of your thought system, first you need to change your mind from focusing on false perceptions based on fear to true perceptions expressing love, which is going from wrong-mindedness to right-mindedness. Then you must work toward enabling your true perceptions to become increasingly unified. Seeing the face of Christ and accepting the Atonement are both means of helping greatly to unify your perceptions. The Atonement "is the one complete concept possible in this world, because it is the source of a wholly unified perception."[92] This unification process is a preparation for final spiritual awakening when all perceptions come together to form "total perception," which is "unified perception that reflects God's knowing."[93] Then when God takes the final step of your awakening, this totally unified perception itself is replaced by the knowledge of Heaven, as dreams disappear and are finally replaced by reality.

Your most effective means of letting go of false fearful perceptions and accepting true loving perceptions is forgiveness. Because the word "healing" is a general term for your one function, the Course provides clarity by saying that your one specific function is forgiveness, since it is your primary means of healing. You practice your one function of forgiveness in this world in order to prepare for your awakening. Workbook Lesson 342 offers this prayer to the Father:

I thank You, Father, for Your plan to save me from the hell I made. It is not real. And You have given me the means to prove its unreality to me. The key is in my hand, and I have reached the door beyond which lies the end of dreams. I stand before the gate of Heaven, wondering if I should enter in and be at home. Let me not wait again today. Let me forgive all things, and let creation be as You would have it be and as it is. Let me remember that I am Your Son, and opening the door at last, forget illusions in the blazing light of truth, as memory of You returns to me.[94]

Seeing the Blazing Light

~ o ~

In the previous prayer, notice the term "**blazing light**." Workbook Lesson 67 teaches the attunement practice of repeating the idea for the day to replace distracting thoughts. It suggests, "Yet perhaps you will succeed in going past that, and through the interval of thoughtlessness to the awareness of a blazing light in which you recognize yourself as love created you."[95] This blazing light is not merely a metaphor, as some would interpret it to be. Rather, it is something actually encountered when you awaken to who you are as God created you.

Although there are many lower levels of seeing the face of Christ identified in the Course, seeing this blazing light is the deepest level. The blazing light describes how the face of Christ truly appears as a vision seen within the mind, not externally with the physical eyes. In one interpretation, the time of passing out of this world when the body is released completely provides the chance to see this blazing light of the face of Christ. If you cannot accept this light and awaken at the end of earthly life, you will be reincarnated. Your reincarnation will give you another lifetime to find awakening, but the Course takes no definitive stand about the belief in reincarnation. Also, the Course does not say that the blazing light helps you to awaken, but it does say that Christ's vision will eventually at some time show you the face of Christ, which must be seen before you can remember your Father and awaken.

But keep in mind that this vision in itself is still not full awakening. It is merely a vision, and the face of Christ remains only a symbol of the real Christ in the Mind of God in Heaven. God Himself must take the final step of carrying you over into Heaven by His grace—beyond visions, beyond perception, and into the full awareness of knowledge, where there is no longer any sense of separation at all. There is only Oneness Perfect Unity in God's Divine Love in Heaven.

Since it is your purpose to awaken, let's address what awakening really means at an experiential level. The concept of awakening is a fundamental idea of Eastern philosophy. In Zen Buddhism the Buddha is considered the Awakened One, and his experience of awakening is called "enlightenment." There are lower levels of enlightenment and higher levels. Examples of the lower level are seeing a tree, looking at a sunset, or hearing a bird chirp and then experiencing a deep sense of oneness. These are examples of joining with what you are experiencing so there is no feeling of separation. There is a sense of being lifted beyond the boundaries of your body. In the Course the statement, "I am not a body. I am free. For I am still as God created me," is repeated twenty times for emphasis. The freedom you feel when the body limitations are lifted is called a "transportation" in the following quotation:

> If you will consider what this "transportation" really entails, you will realize that it is a sudden unawareness of the body, and a joining of yourself and something else in which your mind enlarges to encompass it. It becomes part of you, as you unite with it. And both become whole, as neither is perceived as separate. What really happens is that you have given up the illusion of a limited awareness, and lost your fear of union. The love that instantly replaces it extends to what has freed you, and unites with it. And while this lasts you are not uncertain of your Identity, and would not limit It. You have escaped from fear to peace, asking no questions of reality, but merely accepting it. You have accepted this instead of the body, and have let yourself be one with something beyond it, simply by not letting your mind be limited by it.
>
> This can occur regardless of the physical distance that seems to be between you and what you join; of your respective positions in space; and of your differences in size and seeming quality. Time is not relevant; it can occur with something past, present or anticipated. The "something" can be anything and anywhere; a sound, a sight, a thought, a memory, and even a general idea without specific reference. Yet in every case, you join it without reservation because you love it, and would be with it. And so you rush to meet it, letting your limits melt away, suspending all the "laws" your body obeys and gently setting them aside.[96]

This kind of transportation is the same as what the Zen Buddhists would call a mild experience of enlightenment because it is a sudden experience of oneness, and this oneness can be triggered by anything. The Course does not use the term "enlightenment," but it does say this transportation is similar to what was described previously as the holy instant. "Yet in the holy instant you unite directly with God, and all your brothers join in Christ. Those who are joined in Christ are in no way separate. For Christ is the Self the Sonship shares, as God shares His Self with Christ."[97] This joining with God and with all your brothers that occurs in the holy instant may happen inwardly in meditation, in the joining of a holy relationship, or in other events in daily life. But the vast majority of holy instants that occur are not typically as outwardly dramatic as this transportation, even though there are similarities.

The body is not attacked, but simply properly perceived. It does not limit you, merely because you would not have it so. You are not really "lifted out" of it; it cannot contain you. You go where you would be, gaining, not losing, a sense of Self. In these instants of release from physical restrictions, you experience much of what happens in the holy instant; the lifting of the barriers of time and space, the sudden experience of peace and joy, and, above all, the lack of awareness of the body, and of the questioning whether or not all this is possible.[98]

The Course is making the point that the release of body limitations and the experience of your freedom are directly related. The more you can let go of the body, the more you will experience your freedom. When Zen Buddhists experience the deepest levels of enlightenment, and likewise when Tantric yogis experience the most profound levels of samadhi, the body is released altogether, and there is the greatest experience of freedom, which is always an experience of blazing light. It is the blazing light of awakening, and so that is why the reference in the Course to seeing a blazing light is not a metaphor. Since the body awareness is released, this blazing light is not seen with the physical eyes. It is an inner spiritual vision that is literally seen by the mind. Traditional Christian mysticism uses the word "illumination" to describe the highest vision, which is equivalent to the experience of light in the most profound enlightenment and samadhi.

Only the mind is capable of illumination. Spirit is already illuminated and the body in itself is too dense. The mind, however, can bring its illumination to the body by recognizing that it is not the learner, and is therefore unamenable to learning. The body is, however, easily brought into alignment with a mind that has learned to look beyond it toward the light.[99]

Illumination of the mind is the experience of the blazing light. You join with the light and become one with it in a union of love, but at this point there is still a slight separation, as there is in every vision, because visions are always within the realm of perception, requiring a perceiver and something perceived. Does the Course give a hint as to what this blazing light will look like? It does so in the following passage, which begins with the words "Beyond the body" to show what can be seen when the body is transcended:

Beyond the body, beyond the sun and stars, past everything you see and yet somehow familiar, is an arc of golden light that stretches as you look into a great and shining circle. And all the circle fills with light before your eyes. The edges of the circle disappear, and what is in it is no longer contained at all. The light expands and covers everything, extending to infinity forever shining and with no break or limit anywhere. Within it everything is joined in perfect continuity. Nor is it possible to imagine that anything could be outside, for there is nowhere that this light is not.

This is the vision of the Son of God, whom you know well. Here is the sight of him who knows his Father. Here is the memory of what you are; a part of this, with all of it within, and joined to all as surely as all is joined in you. Accept the vision that can show you this, and not the body.[100]

The last line above indicates again to let go of the body and to accept this vision that is offered to you. Notice the line that says, "This is the vision of the Son of God, whom you know well." Subsequently, there is the line, "Here is the memory of what you are; a part of this, with all of it within, and joined to all as surely as all is joined in you." Thus the seeing of this vision restores your memory of your true Identity. This last sentence can be reworded by inserting the word "Christ" in this way: "Here is the memory of what you are: a part of Christ, with all of the whole Christ within, and joined with all the other parts of Christ as surely as all the other parts of Christ are joined in you." This vision of the Son of God is your call to awaken to your true nature in Christ, Who is within God.

The most important part of the vision itself is the final stage when the edges of the expanding circle disappear, and then: "The light expands and covers everything, extending to infinity forever shining and with no break or limit anywhere." All things are joined in oneness here in "perfect continuity." This is a light that extends to everything and everywhere since it is expanding infinitely. This all-encompassing light cannot be anything other than the blazing light mentioned in a few parts of the Course, and the same blazing light seen by Buddhists in enlightenment and by yogis in samadhi. The Course states: "One thought, completely unified, will serve to unify all thought."[101] This idea is the basis for Eastern meditation defined as the holding of one thought in the mind continuously. Advanced meditators are able to firmly hold one thought to unify the mind. This totally unified perception opens the way for the transcendent experience of the blazing light.

Perceiving True Light

~ ◦ ~

The idea that "**true light**" is a state of mind in which perception is perfectly unified is clarified in the following Course quotation:

> And what is light except the resolution, born of peace, of all your conflicts and mistaken thoughts into one concept which is wholly true? Even that one will disappear, because the Thought behind it will appear instead to take its place. And now you are at peace forever, for the dream is over then.
>
> True light that makes true vision possible is not the light the body's eyes behold. It is a state of mind that has become so unified that darkness cannot be perceived at all. And thus what is the same is seen as one, while what is not the same remains unnoticed, for it is not there.
>
> This is the light that shows no opposites, and vision, being healed, has power to heal. This is the light that brings your peace of mind to other minds, to share it and be glad that they are one with you and with themselves. This is the light that heals because it brings single perception, based upon one frame of reference, from which one meaning comes.[102]

The blazing light is this true light that makes Christ's vision possible. "The wish to see calls down the grace of God upon your eyes, and brings the gift of light that makes sight possible."[103] True light, which is the blazing light, heals, so it must be the source of all the various means of healing, including the Atonement, the face of Christ, miracles, the holy instant, and forgiveness. True light brings peace to the mind along with vision. "Light is tranquility, and in that peace is vision given us, and we can see."[104] Minds appear limited because perception is divided, but in this one true light the mind is so unified that it brings peace and wholeness and thus healing to the teacher of God. This healing is conveyed to other minds producing miracles. The teacher of God may not see the true light inwardly as a vision of blazing light, yet he can still perceive the light within and can extend that light to other minds in miracles. "When a mind has only light, it knows only light. Its own radiance shines all around it, and extends out into the darkness of other minds, transforming them into majesty.[105] The miracle worker can prove to himself that light must be in his mind by the effects of the miracles manifested through him that help himself and others to change their direction—to replace darkness with seeking the awareness of light.

> It may help someone to point out where he is heading, but the point is lost unless he is also helped to change his direction. The unhealed healer cannot do this for him, since he cannot do it for himself. The only meaningful contribution the healer can make is to present an example of one whose direction has been changed *for* him, and who no longer believes in nightmares of any kind. The light in his mind will therefore answer the questioner, who must decide with God that there is light *because* he sees it. And by his acknowledgment the healer knows it is there. That is how perception ultimately is translated into knowledge. The miracle worker begins by perceiving light, and translates his perception into sureness by continually extending it and accepting its acknowledgment. Its effects assure him it is there.[106]

The Course refers to some forms as being neutral, having no inherent content. For example, the body is considered neutral. But light apparently has both form and content. Eastern yoga philosophy speaks of the Light of superconsciousness that transcends all form, yet it also describes a lesser light within form. This lesser light in yoga is called *prana*, which is considered to be a "light substance" that can be acquired but is also considered to be an expression of consciousness itself. The Course never mentions prana, but does say that light has content "since light *is* understanding."[107]

The Course also states: "All thinking produces form at some level."[108] The all-encompassing nature of perfectly unified thinking produces one all-inclusive form at the deepest level. The blazing circle of light expanding infinitely represents the one all-inclusive form at the highest level of the real world of all loving thoughts. This one form contains all other forms in the universe, and so it is the perfect reflection of Heaven. Perceiving this vision is the most profound example of the previously described "transportation." As occurs with all such spiritual experiences, you unite with what you see because you love it. In this case, you join with the light without reservation because you love it and so can experience the freedom of letting go of body limitations. You can make this leap to union, not because of the form of the light, but because of its content. This content is the memory of your own true nature as a Son of God, so you are seeing yourself in this vision. Why do you see yourself in light? The Course states, "Ask for light and learn that you *are* light."[109] You are light because you are a "Son of God, who was created *of* light and *in* light. The Great Light always surrounds you and shines out from you."[110] Normally light is considered to be something distinctly different from the mind. However, in addition to saying, "you *are* light," the Course maintains that God's Light is not in fact different from the mind. "God has lit your mind Himself, and keeps your mind lit by His light because His light is what your mind is."[111]

Apparently there are various kinds of light. At the highest end of the spectrum, there is God's Light, which is the universal Light of Heaven that is totally beyond any element of form. At the lowest end of the spectrum, there is physical light that can be measured within the three-dimensional world. Between these two extremes there is light that has both form and content, and the blazing light is the most exalted expression of this light that has form and content, the content of true perception. Every movement you make away from the ego's thought system and toward the true perception of the real world is a movement away from darkness and toward increasing awareness of light.

> You make by projection, but God creates by extension. The cornerstone of God's creation is you, for His thought system is light. Remember the Rays that are there unseen. The more you approach the center of His thought system, the clearer the light becomes. The closer you come to the foundation of the ego's thought system, the darker and more obscure becomes the way. Yet even the little spark in your mind is enough to lighten it. Bring this light fearlessly with you, and bravely hold it up to the foundation of the ego's thought system.[112]

The description above of moving away from darkness and toward the light is typically interpreted figuratively by most Course scholars. Yet, many such quotations regarding light can also have a literal and mystical interpretation, because the awareness of light increases as the split mind is healed and becomes increasingly unified. The Course describes a variety of different ways in which the awareness of inner light becomes increasingly apparent.

> As we go along, you may have many "light episodes." They may take many different forms, some of them quite unexpected. Do not be afraid of them. They are signs that you are opening your eyes at last. They will not persist, because they merely symbolize true perception, and they are not related to knowledge. These exercises will not reveal knowledge to you. But they will prepare the way to it.[113]

The key points here are that these light experiences are temporary and do not represent knowledge. They are within the realm of form, and they are symbols of the true perception that is in the mind of each seeker who experiences this light. They are not expressions of the knowledge or the light of Heaven. But they are reflections of the divine light of Heaven, just as true perceptions themselves are loving reflection of the Love of God in Heaven. These light experiences are not knowledge, but they prepare the way for the acceptance of knowledge and the acceptance of Heaven. They are signs that the split mind is becoming increasingly healed, which is the preparation for the dawning of knowledge. When that process of unifying the split mind is complete at the perceptual level, the result is a universal experience of light, which is recognized in every traditional mystical religion. The Course clearly acknowledges the great importance of this universal experience in the following quotation: "A universal theology is impossible, but a universal experience is not only possible but necessary. It is this experience toward which the course is directed."[114] This universal experience is the ultimate temporary "light episode" that occurs when the mind is healed by unified perception, prior to the advent of knowledge when the mind becomes completely whole in Heaven. This universal experience is the vision of this blazing light, which produces a temporary awakening that occurs one step before the final awakening in Heaven. All world mystical traditions and philosophies lead to here, although the words used to describe it vary greatly.

Oneness of Ideas
Leading to Awakening

≈ • ≈

As was already noted, the Course uses many lofty terms that overlap and meet in one purpose as a reflection of Heaven. Here is a clear example: "Forgiveness, salvation, Atonement, true perception, all are one. They are the one beginning, with the end to lead to oneness far beyond themselves."[115] The blazing light can be added to these names that symbolize the road to oneness and lead beyond themselves to Heaven. The blazing light may be thought of as the one reflection of Heaven that transcends all the other reflections of Heaven. All the reflections of Heaven meet in one place, which is this blazing light that is the vision of the Son of God. This place is "always" because it is the one holy instant that contains all other holy instants in time. This place is "all ways" because it is the one space that contains all of space itself. All the forms in the universe are within its infinitely expanding light. Futhermore, this blazing light is the one miracle that contains all other seemingly different miracles. This all-encompassing reflection of Heaven is the final happy dream in which all your other dreams of the world and time will finally disappear.

The blazing light is the home of the Atonement, which "is the one complete concept possible in this world, because it is the source of a wholly unified perception."[116] The Atonement literally dwells in the blazing light. "The Atonement is entirely unambiguous. It is perfectly clear because it exists in light."[117] Apparently accepting the Atonement involves activating the blazing light referred to as the "inner light" in this quotation: "The Atonement can only be accepted within you by releasing the inner light."[118] Thus the blazing light gives the Atonement the power to correct all mistakes in time and yet builds the bridge beyond time to timelessness. "Until the Atonement is complete, its various phases will proceed in time, but the whole Atonement stands at time's end. At that point the bridge of return has been built."[119]

The blazing light is total perception, meaning unified perception, including all of the real world that contains only loving perceptions. It is this total perception that is so unified that it is one step away from the knowledge of Heaven and makes the transfer to full awakening possible. "Perception is not knowledge, but it can be transferred to knowledge, or cross over into it."[120] This blazing light consisting of total perception is what the Course calls the "**holy meeting place**"[121] where God comes to take His Son back to Heaven.

One very significant aspect of the blazing light is that it is the "quiet light in which the Holy Spirit dwells."[122] Before considering how the blazing light can be so many-faceted and yet be one, it is necessary to consider the nature of the Holy Spirit. The dual nature of the Holy Spirit is this: He knows because He is an aspect of God, and He perceives because He was sent to save humanity. The Holy Spirit possesses the **One-mindedness** of Heaven, which is another name for the total awareness of knowledge. The Holy Spirit also contains all the loving true perceptions of right-mindedness. The first goal of the Holy Spirit is to help you to make the transition from the fearful false perceptions of wrong-mindedness to the loving true perceptions of right-mindedness. The second goal of the Holy Spirit is to bring together the many different true perceptions of your mind and move them in the direction of oneness. This unification of true perceptions is not the One-mindedness of Heaven, but it leads to total perception and then makes the transfer to knowledge possible. Even though Jesus is considered the Author of the Course, the Holy Spirit is speaking through Jesus in the Course. Thus it should not be surprising that so many of the spiritual concepts in the Course are interrelated and lead all in one direction—toward the oneness that will eventually become One-mindedness. The total healing of the split mind is attained in One-mindedness and is your awakening that is the third and final goal of the Holy Spirit.

A More Thorough
Interpretation

~ ◦ ~

In the section titled "Why Study the Course?" at the beginning of this overview, you were introduced to the "horse-of-a-different-color" analogy. If you think it would be helpful, you might want to reread that section to remind yourself about the interpretation of this analogy.

Now let's examine this analogy in much greater detail. Your friend in this analogy is the Holy Spirit, Who tells you that the photos you see of the world through the camera of your body's eyes are distorted images manufactured by your split mind. After you see that some images of the world are distorted, you then generalize your learning to realize that everything your physical eyes show you is a distortion of reality. In the analogy your acceptance of your friend's plan to correct all the distortions is symbolic of your acceptance of the Holy Spirit's plan called the Atonement, which corrects all errors of the split mind. Also, in the analogy your using of your friend's gift of a photo editing program to transform the photographic images is symbolic of your using the Holy Spirit's gift of Christ's vision. Just as the photo editing program removes the distortions in the photographs in the analogy, Christ's vision removes the distortions produced by false perception. The Holy Spirit's gift of Christ's vision allows you to use true perception and transform your seeing of the world and other people.

Perceiving the photos in the analogy as black and white images symbolically represents distinguishing between false perceptions and true perceptions, between images of fear and images of love. In the analogy as you gaze at the pictures, you overlook all the black and grey parts of the background, and you look only at the white image of the horse. This overlooking and looking symbolizes forgiveness in which you overlook the dark false perceptions of sin, fear, and guilt, and you look for the true perceptions that display divine reflections of light and love. In the analogy you generalize your seeing of the many photos of the white horse to realize you are seeing the same horse—one horse viewed from different angles. Similarly, you generalize your experience of Christ's vision to learn that you are seeing the image of the same one divine presence in every person and in every object in the world. In the analogy, you looked at the very clear close-up photo of the white face of the horse. Then you remembered that you had previously seen this particular white horse before since it was owned by your friend. The close-up photo of the white face of the horse, of course, symbolizes the seeing of the face of Christ, which brings back to your mind the memory of God that had been hidden, but not entirely lost. In the analogy, to confirm your memory that this is indeed your friend's horse, your friend shows you his real white horse that had been depicted in the photographs. Likewise, your Friend, the Holy Spirit, brings you to the face of Christ, and God takes the final step of revealing to you His Reality beyond all images. In the final part of the analogy, you could see how beautiful the real horse is, and you embrace the white horse. Just as you love to see the beauty of the real white horse and embrace him in the analogy, you love to see the beauty of God, Who Himself is Ultimate Reality. You merge with Him, melting into His Love with a divine embrace that raises you back to your true Home in Heaven.

That is the full detailed explanation of the horse analogy, but here is the nutshell alternative version:

Many of the true perceptions in the Course appear at least initially to be distinctly different spiritual principles, like the colored photos in the horse analogy. But these seemingly different spiritual concepts are completely interrelated and interconnected, and they are all moving in just one coordinated direction. Just as the pictures in the analogy are of the same perfectly white horse, the Course is holding out to you just one image with one meaning, which encompasses all other images and all other lesser meanings. What is this one meaning? It is the meaning of Oneness, which returns your memory of God. What is this one image that contains one meaning? It is the image of the blazing and perfectly white light, which is within form because it is not the light of Heaven itself. Yet the blazing white light is the one form, the one image, that leads to the formlessness of Reality itself beyond all images.

The Holy Spirit
has taken Form

~ o ~

Just what does the Holy Spirit have to do with form? The knowing part of the Holy Spirit resides in the formlessness of the Christ Mind. Where does the perceiving part of the Holy Spirit reside? According to the Course, the Holy Spirit, as the Voice for God, has "taken form. This form is not His reality...."[123] The Holy Spirit has taken the form of the blazing light. Although all form must be illusory, this one illusory form that the Holy Spirit has taken leads beyond all illusions to reality. The transcendent nature of reality is far beyond human perceptual understanding, so the Holy Spirit uses various symbols that are pictures of reality, like the pictures of the horses taken from different angles with a camera having different colored filters. It is altogether fitting that the Holy Spirit, as the facilitator for unification, has taken the form of the one symbol that encompasses and transcends all other symbols of reality. This one symbol is the blazing white light represented in the horse analogy as the one perfectly white horse that is depicted in the form of pictures to symbolize the reality of the white horse itself.

Let's look at how form itself was made. Scientists can accurately measure the expansion of the universe and thus calculate the time when this expansion first began in the explosion called the Big Bang, but their calculations cannot to go back any further in time than that instant. This is not surprising since the Big Bang was the start of the separation and the beginning of both time and space, which did not exist in the formlessness of Heaven. In the same instant of the separation and the Big Bang, God created the Holy Spirit as the Answer to the separation. The instant the Holy Spirit was created, He took on the form of the blazing light expanding infinitely as His response to the explosion of the Big Bang, when form itself was created as an expression of division. The blazing light of the Holy Spirit became the one unifying form that overlapped and encompassed all the separated forms of the universe that were the result of the Big Bang. At the content level, the Holy Spirit taking on the form of the blazing light became the one perfectly unified true perception that contained total perception of all loving thought.

Even though the Big Bang brought forth the picture of a universe of separate forms, the Holy Spirit as the blazing light became the divine response—the picture of union, the doorway of return from separation back to the oneness of Heaven.

Although the Holy Spirit dwells in "quiet light," which can be none other than the blazing light, the Course goes a step further to say that the Holy Spirit *is* light in this way: "He is the light in which the forgiven world is perceived; in which the face of Christ alone is seen."[124] The Holy Spirit's light is identified as the Call to wake up the sleeping Sons of God: "His light is always the Call to awaken, whatever you have been dreaming. Nothing lasting lies in dreams, and the Holy Spirit, shining with the light from God Himself, speaks only for what lasts forever."[125] With the light from God shining in Him and through Him, the Holy Spirit directs His divine influence toward the one goal of bringing about awakening. The Holy Spirit facilitates awakening in a wide variety of ways, since "He is the great correction principle; the bringer of true perception, the inherent power of the vision of Christ."[126]

The most important practical way the Holy Spirit helps you awaken is by offering you Christ's vision. Through this vision given to you by the Holy Spirit, you can see light and Christ in your brothers and sisters. Thus you learn indirectly that light and Christ must be within you as well. You are always choosing between the Holy Spirit and the ego, between sinlessness and sinfulness, and between love and fear. Christ's vision allows you to practice forgiveness—to overlook the ego, sinfulness, and fear and look for the Holy Spirit, sinlessness, and love. In the following four paragraphs, notice that light makes Christ's vision possible and that the Holy Spirit Himself is this light, identified as "the Light in which Christ stands revealed."

> Vision depends on light. You cannot see in darkness. Yet in darkness, in the private world of sleep, you see in dreams although your eyes are closed. And it is here that what you see you made. But let the darkness go and all you made you will no longer see, for sight of it depends upon denying vision. Yet from denying vision it does not follow you cannot see. But this is what denial does, for by it you accept insanity, believing you can make a private world and rule your own perception. Yet for this, light must be excluded. Dreams disappear when light has come and you can see.
>
> Do not seek vision through your eyes, for you made your way of seeing that you might see in darkness, and in this you

are deceived. Beyond this darkness, and yet still within you, is the vision of Christ, Who looks on all in light. Your "vision" comes from fear, as His from love. And He sees for you, as your witness to the real world. He is the Holy Spirit's manifestation, looking always on the real world, and calling forth its witnesses and drawing them to you. He loves what He sees within you, and He would extend it. And He will not return unto the Father until He has extended your perception even unto Him. And there perception is no more, for He has returned you to the Father with Him.

You have but two emotions [love and fear], and one [fear] you made and one [love] was given you [by God]. Each is a way of seeing, and different worlds arise from their different sights. See through the vision that is given you, for through Christ's vision He beholds Himself. And seeing what He is, He knows His Father. Beyond your darkest dreams He sees God's guiltless Son within you, shining in perfect radiance that is undimmed by your dreams. And this *you* will see as you look with Him, for His vision is His gift of love to you, given Him of the Father for you.

The Holy Spirit is the light in which Christ stands revealed. And all who would behold Him can see Him, for they have asked for light. Nor will they see Him alone, for He is no more alone than they are. Because they saw the Son, they have risen in Him to the Father. And all this will they understand, because they looked within and saw beyond the darkness the Christ in them, and recognized Him. In the sanity of His vision they looked upon themselves with love, seeing themselves as the Holy Spirit sees them. And with this vision of the truth in them came all the beauty of the world to shine upon them.[127]

Christ's vision is presented many times in the Course as your means of seeing the divine in your brother, which only indirectly enables you to perceive the divine within yourself. Yet this indirect vision is merely a preparation for the ultimate vision of the Son of God, which happens when you see the blazing light that directly reveals the perfect image of your own true nature in God. When the Holy Spirit became "the Light in which Christ stands revealed" and took on the form of the blazing light at the time of the separation, there was no name yet assigned to that light. Now there are many names used to describe the various aspects of this unifying light. It can be called the source of the real world, the forgiven world, the Atonement, and Christ's vision. Most Course scholars would disagree with this interpretation of the infinite light as it is described in the vision of the Son of God. They would say that the reference to this universal light is only a metaphor. But anyone who has had the experience of the blazing light will affirm that this infinitely expanding and blazing light can be interpreted literally. The experience of the blazing light is so dynamic and compelling that it creates an indelible impression in the mind and removes all doubt about its universal nature.

Furthermore, the vision of Christ is the same as the vision of the deepest level of the face of Christ. At the form level, they are both the single image of the blazing light. At the content level, the light-filled vision of the Son of God returns your memory of your true Identity in Christ and in God. This content is really no different than the highest level of seeing the vision of the face of Christ in the real world that must be seen before the memory of God returns. Since the face of Christ is not Christ, but only a perfect image of Christ, what image other than infinitely expanding light could better represent this picture of Christ? One Course reference to the face of Christ refers to "the bright Rays of His Father's Love that light His [Christ's] face with glory."[128] Another passage states that Christ's "radiance shines through each body that it looks upon, and brushes all its darkness into light merely by looking past it *to* the light. The veil is lifted through its gentleness, and nothing hides the face of Christ from its beholders."[129] When no outer forms of bodies or thoughts of guilt obscure your Christ's vision of your brother, the veil before the face of Christ is lifted to reveal the light of the vision of the Son of God. Perhaps the strongest case for identifying the vision of the Son of God with the face of Christ is the following passage which refers to "the blazing light upon the altar to the Son of God" while also saying "the face of Christ has shone away time's final instant" as the memory of God returns when He takes the final step of transformation:

And now God's *knowledge*, changeless, certain, pure and wholly understandable, enters its kingdom. Gone is perception, false and true alike. Gone is forgiveness, for its task is done. And gone are bodies in the blazing light upon the altar to the Son of God. God knows it is His Own, as it is his. And here They join, for here the face of Christ has shone away time's final instant, and now is the last perception of the world without a purpose and without a cause. For where God's memory has come at last there is no journey, no belief in sin, no walls, no bodies, and the grim appeal of guilt and death is there snuffed out forever.[130]

Content is More
Important than Form

~ ◦ ~

In spite of the implications of the preceding quote, there is a reason why the Course does not want to directly state that the experience of seeing the infinitely expanding light in the vision of the Son of God is the same as seeing the deepest level of the face of Christ. The reason is that the Course does not want you to focus on the phenomenon of the visual experience, even an inner spiritual vision such as this one, which is seen without the body's eyes. The Course always emphasizes content over any form, even this most exalted phenomenon of light expanding limitlessly. The Course wants you to focus on the underlying meaning, the content of forgiveness, which the face of Christ symbolizes, because that is what is practical for your daily life and relationships.

In Zen Buddhism and Tantric yoga, the sole prize is for the individual seeker to have the direct experience of the transcendental light. The Course calls the direct experience of God by the term "revelation" and says it cannot be expressed in words because "it is an experience of unspeakable love."[131] Certainly through a great deal of devotion and dedication, a teacher of God may experience this unspeakable love as a momentary glimpse of the final end of his journey. "Sometimes a teacher of God may have a brief experience of direct union with God."[132] Although this direct awakening and union with God is a possibility, the Course is quick to firmly point out that the experience of revelation is "so rare that it cannot be considered a realistic goal."[133] Revelation temporarily produces the experience of the total awareness of knowledge, which opens a window to the natural spiritual condition of Heaven. "Knowledge is the result of revelation and induces only thought."[134] However, the total knowledge of Heaven is not applicable to navigating through the world of everyday perceptions where partial awareness is needed to correct the errors of the split mind. In the Course Jesus says, "As a man I did not attempt to counteract error with knowledge, but to correct error from the bottom up."[135] In other words, the errors of the ego must be corrected at the level of perception, where they occur. "The Holy Spirit has the task of undoing what the ego has made. He undoes it at the same level on which the ego operates, or the mind would be unable to understand the change."[136]

Instead of seeking the very lofty experience of revelation and the total knowledge that comes with it, the Course recommends setting the more attainable goal of performing miracles that change perception and that produce results in the world, The reason is that miracles "are more useful [than revelation] because of their interpersonal nature."[137]

The Course consistently recommends seeking God through finding Him in other people, as is the case with miracles. "Miracles, however, are genuinely interpersonal, and result in true closeness to others. Revelation unites you directly with God. Miracles unite you directly with your brother."[138] This experience of uniting with your brothers and sisters is also what happens in the holy instant.

Just as the Course does not recommend actively seeking revelation, it does not emphasize setting the goal of seeing the face of Christ as a direct inner experience for the benefit of you alone. Instead, the Course presents a much easier path based on finding God in interpersonal relations. Thus the Course is a practical training program for healing the split mind by gaining Christ's vision that enables you to see the face of Christ everywhere in your daily life. Through Christ's vision the face of Christ can be seen everywhere, even in ordinary objects such as a table in the example below:

> You could, in fact, gain vision from just that table, if you would withdraw all your own ideas from it, and look upon it with a completely open mind. It has something to show you; something beautiful and clean and of infinite value, full of happiness and hope.[139]

Of course, the face of Christ can most easily be seen in your brothers and sisters if you can learn to see them without judging them. Just as you can learn to see beauty and purity in an ordinary table, you can learn to see the divine truth in your brother that you normally overlook. "And in Christ's vision is his loveliness reflected in a form so holy and so beautiful that you could scarce refrain from kneeling at his feet."[140] Studying the Text, doing the daily Workbook lessons, and becoming a teacher of God are all means of obtaining the vision of the face of Christ. This is a slow step-by-step learning process in which you see more and more of the face of Christ as you perform your single function of forgiveness. What will your forgiveness reveal to you?

> Can you imagine how beautiful those you forgive will look to you? In no fantasy have you ever seen anything so lovely. Nothing you see here, sleeping or waking, comes near to such

loveliness. And nothing will you value like unto this, nor hold so dear. Nothing that you remember that made your heart sing with joy has ever brought you even a little part of the happiness this sight will bring you. For you will see the Son of God. You will behold the beauty the Holy Spirit loves to look upon, and which He thanks the Father for. He was created to see this for you, until you learned to see it for yourself. And all His teaching leads to seeing it and giving thanks with Him.

This loveliness is not a fantasy. It is the real world, bright and clean and new, with everything sparkling under the open sun. Nothing is hidden here, for everything has been forgiven and there are no fantasies to hide the truth.[141]

It is hard to believe love and holiness is within you because of so much past conditioning that seems to prove otherwise. When you seek the divine only within yourself alone, it is hard to believe in your perfection in Christ that is your true Self. However, it is easier to see goodness in others who become mirrors in which you can see your own goodness reflected. First you must learn to practice forgiveness of your brother in order to facilitate healing. Forgiveness allows you to express **charity**, which "is a way of perceiving the perfection of another even if you cannot perceive it in yourself."[142] Below is one example of a Workbook lesson that teaches you how to be charitable to your brother. You are asked to "think of someone you do not like" and then are given these instructions.

> Try to perceive some light in him somewhere; a little gleam which you had never noticed. Try to find some little spark of brightness shining through the ugly picture that you hold of him. Look at this picture till you see a light somewhere within it, and then try to let this light extend until it covers him, and makes the picture beautiful and good.
>
> Look at this changed perception for a while, and turn your mind to one you call a friend. Try to transfer the light you learned to see around your former "enemy" to him. Perceive him now as more than friend to you, for in that light his holiness shows you your savior, saved and saving, healed and whole.
>
> Then let him offer you the light you see in him, and let your "enemy" and friend unite in blessing you with what you gave. Now are you one with them, and they with you. Now have you been forgiven by yourself.[143]

Light and Forgiveness Lead to Awakening

~ • ~

This overview of the Course has paid a great deal of attention to the role of light in the process of spiritual growth, even though forgiveness is the central theme of the Course itself. The emphasis on light is not just lofty philosophy. Yes, the blazing light of the face of Christ is waiting for your acceptance, and God's Light is waiting for your embrace in Heaven. Yet the light is not just waiting for you at the last steps of your journey. The light is with you *now* every step of the way along your road to awakening. This entire book is for the beginner, who is likely to underestimate the practical value and accessibility of light. The only thing required of you is openness. The light is a central focus here in order to inform you that the light is available to you and to encourage you to call upon the light. In your inner seeking of meditation, you can open your mind to welcome the light. You do not have to see light to welcome it. You can simply ask the Holy Spirit to enlighten your mind. The light can be sensed; it can be felt through opening your mind to it. Likewise, the light can be sensed and felt in your practice of forgiveness.

Notice that the previous workbook lesson asks you to perceive light in your brother. Perceiving light is not merely a poetic description without any practical application. Just as light can be sensed and felt inwardly in meditation, it can also be sensed and felt in your mind in your practical application of forgiveness. While you are practicing your short-term goal of forgiveness in your daily life, it is very helpful to simultaneously keep in mind your long-term goal of awakening to divine light. In forgiveness you overlook all outer forms and look for the divine in others. Looking for light in your brother is an excellent means of succeeding in forgiveness. Why? Because there is in fact light in your brother since he *is* light. Seeing him as he really is in the light reminds you that you *are* light as much as he is. A miracle of love happens in this forgiveness in which light actually goes from your mind, which is light, to his mind, which is light. In gratitude, the mind of the forgiven person will transmit light back to you. This exchange of light and love happens literally, not just figuratively. You may not be able to actually feel the movement of light, but you can see its effects on the one you forgive, and you can feel the effect of peace that it brings within your own mind. Opening to light is the same as opening to love and holiness because they are one and always go together. Opening to love will also bring light and holiness, just as opening to holiness will also bring light and love. This opening of yourself is easy and joyful to do because you are simply accepting the light, love, and holiness that are already within you as your true nature.

Forgiveness allows you to overlook what outer appearances would tell you about your brother. Forgiveness enables you to use charity as "a way of looking at another as if he had already gone far beyond his actual accomplishments in time."[144] Seeing your brother through charity will lead to your awakening.

> Dream softly of your sinless brother, who unites with you in holy innocence. And from this dream the Lord of Heaven will Himself awaken His beloved Son. Dream of your brother's kindnesses instead of dwelling in your dreams on his mistakes. Select his thoughtfulness to dream about instead of counting up the hurts he gave. Forgive him his illusions, and give thanks to him for all the helpfulness he gave. And do not brush aside his many gifts because he is not perfect in your dreams.... Let all your brother's gifts be seen in light of charity and kindness offered you. And let no pain disturb your dream of deep appreciation for his gifts to you.[145]

Perceiving the goodness in your bother strengthens the belief in your own goodness. "What you acknowledge in your brother you are acknowledging in yourself, and what you share you strengthen."[146] Your giving of charity helps you to be charitable in your perception of yourself, and you begin to believe in your own true nature in Christ. "Your holy Son is pointed out to me, first in my brother; then in me."[147] Your brother becomes your savior because through seeing his loveliness and holiness as a Son of God, you claim your own loveliness and holiness as a Son of God. But if you want to eventually accept the divine love that is within you, you must not leave anyone outside the acceptance of your forgiving eyes.

> You cannot enter into real relationships with any of God's Sons unless you love them all and equally. Love is not special. If you single out part of the Sonship for your love, you are imposing guilt on all your relationships and making them unreal. You can love only as God loves. Seek not to love unlike Him, for there is no love apart from His.[148]

Through learning to apply forgiveness equally to all of your brothers and sisters on a consistent basis and through establishing and nourishing holy relationships, you will eventually see the real world and the face of Christ at the deepest level of the real world where there are only loving thoughts. Your world of nightmares will be changed to the happy dream that becomes your bridge to Heaven. The Course clearly identifies the certainty of reaching your final destination, which is a joyful return to the Heart of God. Yet that lofty long-term goal of full awakening is not the primary focus of the Course, which remains steadfastly focused on your means of transforming your everyday life and relationships by practicing forgiveness. God will most certainly do His part of taking the final step of bringing you to Heaven, as long as you do your part of preparing yourself by consistently expressing forgiveness throughout your life. The entire Course is directed toward helping you learn how to heal your split mind by manifesting a life of forgiveness. The Course does not attempt to exceed this simple goal of forgiveness because when forgiveness is complete, all else is provided by divine grace. Forgiveness merely removes all the obstacles that would obscure seeing the face of Christ, which in turn leads to awakening.

No clouds remain to hide the face of Christ. Now is the goal achieved. Forgiveness is the final goal of the curriculum. It paves the way for what goes far beyond all learning. The curriculum makes no effort to exceed its legitimate goal. Forgiveness is its single aim, at which all learning ultimately converges. It is indeed enough.[149]

The Simplicity
of the Course

≈ • ≈

How simple the Course is! You are not being asked to accomplish an extraordinary spiritual feat like the Buddha sitting in superhuman one-pointed meditation and becoming enlightened. You are not being asked to surrender your life on the cross as Jesus did in order to be resurrected and become the light of the world. The Course simply asks you to implement forgiveness. Transforming your thought system requires intellectually understanding forgiveness and the many Course ideas supporting it. Yet, rather than promoting theory alone, the emphasis in the Course is on application. Consequently, the direct practice of forgiveness is the heart of the Course, which teaches you, *"Forgiveness is my function as the light of the world. I would fulfill my function that I may be happy."*[150]

Your ego can give you pride that overestimates your abilities, but your ego is much more likely to misguide you by encouraging you to invest in littleness. You think your mind is small and the world is vast, so you think you could never be the light of the world. You ask: "How could forgiveness possibly make me the light of the world?" The truth is that your mind is so all-encompassing that the entire world is *within* it, just as your mind is within the Mind of God. As you perform your function of forgiveness, you bring light to your brother's mind and to your own mind. You also bring light to the world that is in your mind, and through the Holy Spirit your miracle of forgiveness brings light to every Son of God in the Sonship. "A miracle is never lost. It may touch many people you have not even met, and produce undreamed of changes in situations of which you are not even aware."[151] The Course says, "Your mission is very simple. You are asked to live so as to demonstrate that you are not an ego...."[152] This would be difficult except that the Course gives you an easy means of accomplishing your mission. Forgiveness allows you to overcome the ego, not by attacking it, but by looking past it to your brother and joining with him in the light. Your joining proves there is no separation, and therefore the ego has lost its foundation.

What is your ultimate return for your offerings of forgiveness? There is one glorious moment awaiting you in time that will bring timelessness. You can bring this time closer to you every time you practice true forgiveness advocated by the Course. Or you can take a direction away from forgiveness and delay the coming of this time. Whether you turn right or left can only hasten or delay the date, but it is absolutely certain that this day of awakening will come eventually. The glorious time is inevitable because it is God's Will for you and your own true will for yourself. What will this time be like when the light suddenly and fully dawns again illuminating your mind?

> O my child, if you knew what God wills for you, your joy would be complete! And what He wills has happened, for it was always true. When the light comes and you have said, "God's Will is mine," you will see such beauty that you will know it is not of you. Out of your joy you will create beauty in His Name, for your joy could no more be contained than His. The bleak little world will vanish into nothingness, and your heart will be so filled with joy that it will leap into Heaven, and into the Presence of God. I cannot tell you what this will be like, for your heart is not ready. Yet I can tell you, and remind you often, that what God wills for Himself He wills for you, and what He wills for you is yours.[153]

Quotes that Summarize
"A Course in Miracles"

≈ ∘ ≈

In the latter portion of the Course's Workbook, there are fourteen questions that are asked. Each question is answered with a full page of text. In the passages below, each answer has been reduced in size to a few paragraphs. The following six pages of direct quotations from the Workbook form a brief summary of the principles of the Course:

1. WHAT IS FORGIVENESS?

Forgiveness recognizes what you thought your brother did to you has not occurred. It does not pardon sins and make them real. It sees there was no sin. And in that view are all your sins forgiven. What is sin, except a false idea about God's Son? Forgiveness merely sees its falsity, and therefore lets it go. What then is free to take its place is now the Will of God.[154]

2. WHAT IS SALVATION?

Salvation is a promise, made by God, that you would find your way to Him at last. It cannot but be kept. It guarantees that time will have an end, and all the thoughts that have been born in time will end as well. God's Word is given every mind which thinks that it has separate thoughts, and will replace these thoughts of conflict with the Thought of peace.

The Thought of peace was given to God's Son the instant that his mind had thought of war. There was no need for such a Thought before, for peace was given without opposite, and merely was. But when the mind is split there is a need of healing. So the Thought that has the power to heal the split became a part of every fragment of the mind that still was one, but failed to recognize its oneness. Now it did not know itself, and thought its own Identity was lost.[155]

3. WHAT IS THE WORLD?

The world is false perception. It is born of error, and it has not left its source. It will remain no longer than the thought that gave it birth is cherished. When the thought of separation has been changed to one of true forgiveness, will the world be seen in quite another light; and one which leads to truth, where all the world must disappear and all its errors vanish. Now its source has gone, and its effects are gone as well.

The world was made as an attack on God. It symbolizes fear. And what is fear except love's absence? Thus the world was meant to be a place where God could enter not, and where His Son could be apart from Him. Here was perception born, for knowledge could not cause such insane thoughts. But eyes deceive, and ears hear falsely. Now mistakes become quite possible, for certainty has gone.[156]

4. WHAT IS SIN?

Sin is the home of all illusions, which but stand for things imagined, issuing from thoughts that are untrue. They are the "proof" that what has no reality is real. Sin "proves" God's Son is evil; timelessness must have an end; eternal life must die. And God Himself has lost the Son He loves, with but corruption to complete Himself, His Will forever overcome by death, love slain by hate, and peace to be no more.

A madman's dreams are frightening, and sin appears indeed to terrify. And yet what sin perceives is but a childish game. The Son of God may play he has become a body, prey to evil and to guilt, with but a little life that ends in death. But all the while his Father shines on him, and loves him with an everlasting Love which his pretenses cannot change at all.[157]

5. WHAT IS THE BODY?

The body is a dream. Like other dreams it sometimes seems to picture happiness, but can quite suddenly revert to fear, where every dream is born. For only love creates in truth, and truth can never fear. Made to be fearful, must the body serve the purpose given it. But we can change the purpose that the body will obey by changing what we think that it is for.

The body is the means by which God's Son returns to sanity. Though it was made to fence him into hell without escape, yet has the goal of Heaven been exchanged for the pursuit of hell. The Son of God extends his hand to reach his brother, and to help him walk along the road with him. Now is the body holy. Now it serves to heal the mind that it was made to kill.

You will identify with what you think will make you safe. Whatever it may be, you will believe that it is one with you. Your safety lies in truth, and not in lies. Love is your safety. Fear does not exist. Identify with love, and you are safe. Identify with love, and you are home. Identify with love, and find your Self.[158]

6. WHAT IS THE CHRIST?

Christ is God's Son as He created Him. He is the Self we share, uniting us with one another, and with God as well. He is the Thought which still abides within the Mind that is His Source. He has not left His holy home, nor lost the innocence in which He was created. He abides unchanged forever in the Mind of God.

Christ is the link that keeps you one with God, and guarantees that separation is no more than an illusion of despair, for hope forever will abide in Him. Your mind is part of His, and His of yours. He is the part in which God's Answer lies; where all decisions are already made, and dreams are over. He remains untouched by anything the body's eyes perceive. For though in Him His Father placed the means for your salvation, yet does He remain the Self Who, like His Father, knows no sin.[159]

7. WHAT IS THE HOLY SPIRIT?

The Holy Spirit mediates between illusions and the truth. Since He must bridge the gap between reality and dreams, perception leads to knowledge through the grace that God has given Him, to be His gift to everyone who turns to Him for truth. Across the bridge that He provides are dreams all carried to the truth, to be dispelled before the light of knowledge. There are sights and sounds forever laid aside. And where they were perceived before, forgiveness has made possible perception's tranquil end.

The goal the Holy Spirit's teaching sets is just this end of dreams. For sights and sounds must be translated from the witnesses of fear to those of love. And when this is entirely accomplished, learning has achieved the only goal it has in truth. For learning, as the Holy Spirit guides it to the outcome He perceives for it, becomes the means to go beyond itself, to be replaced by the eternal truth.[160]

8. WHAT IS THE REAL WORLD?

The real world is a symbol, like the rest of what perception offers. Yet it stands for what is opposite to what you made. Your world is seen through eyes of fear, and brings the witnesses of terror to your mind. The real world cannot be perceived except through eyes forgiveness blesses, so they see a world where terror is impossible, and witnesses to fear can not be found.

The real world is the symbol that the dream of sin and guilt is over, and God's Son no longer sleeps. His waking *eyes* perceive the sure reflection of his Father's Love; the certain promise that he is redeemed. The real world signifies the end of time, for its perception makes time purposeless.

The Holy Spirit has no need of time when it has served His purpose. Now He waits but that one instant more for God to take His final step, and time has disappeared, taking perception with it as it goes, and leaving but the truth to be itself. That instant is our goal, for it contains the memory of God. And as we look upon a world forgiven, it is He Who calls to us and comes to take us home, reminding us of our Identity which our forgiveness has restored to us.[161]

9. WHAT IS THE SECOND COMING?

Christ's Second Coming, which is sure as God, is merely the correction of mistakes, and the return of sanity. It is a part of the condition that restores the never lost, and re-establishes what is forever and forever true. It is the invitation to God's Word to take illusion's place; the willingness to let forgiveness rest upon all things without exception and without reserve.

The Second Coming is the one event in time which time itself can not affect. For every one who ever came to die, or yet will come or who is present now, is equally released from what he made. In this equality is Christ restored as one Identity, in which the Sons of God acknowledge that they all are one. And God the Father smiles upon His Son, His one creation and His only joy.[162]

10. WHAT IS THE LAST JUDGMENT?

You who believed that God's Last Judgment would condemn the world to hell along with you, accept this holy truth: God's Judgment is the gift of the Correction He bestowed on all your errors, freeing you from them, and all effects they ever seemed to have. To fear God's saving grace is but to fear complete release from suffering, return to peace, security and happiness, and union with your own Identity.

This is God's Final Judgment: "You are still My holy Son, forever innocent, forever loving and forever loved, as limitless as your Creator, and completely changeless and forever pure. Therefore awaken and return to Me. I am your Father and you are My Son."[163]

11. WHAT IS CREATION?

Creation is the opposite of all illusions, for creation is the truth. Creation is the holy Son of God, for in creation is His Will complete in every aspect, making every part container of the whole. Its oneness is forever guaranteed inviolate; forever held within His holy Will, beyond all possibility of harm, of separation, imperfection and of any spot upon its sinlessness.

We are creation; we the Sons of God. We seem to be discrete, and unaware of our eternal unity with Him. Yet back of all our doubts, past all our fears, there still is certainty. For love remains with all its Thoughts, its sureness being theirs. God's memory is in our holy minds, which know their oneness and their unity with their Creator. Let our function be only to let this memory return, only to let God's Will be done on earth, only to be restored to sanity, and to be but as God created us.

Our Father calls to us. We hear His Voice, and we forgive creation in the Name of its Creator, Holiness Itself, Whose Holiness His Own creation shares; Whose Holiness is still a part of us.[164]

12. WHAT IS THE EGO?

The ego is insane. In fear it stands beyond the Everywhere, apart from All, in separation from the Infinite. In its insanity it thinks it has become a victor over God Himself. And in its terrible autonomy it "sees" the Will of God has been destroyed. It dreams of punishment, and trembles at the figures in its dreams; its enemies, who seek to murder it before it can ensure its safety by attacking them.

Yet will one lily of forgiveness change the darkness into light; the altar to illusions to the shrine of Life Itself. And peace will be restored forever to the holy minds which God created as His Son, His dwelling place, His joy, His love, completely His, completely one with Him.[165]

13. WHAT IS A MIRACLE?

A miracle is a correction. It does not create, nor really change at all. It merely looks on devastation, and reminds the mind that what it sees is false. It undoes error, but does not attempt to go beyond perception, nor exceed the function of forgiveness. Thus it stays within time's limits. Yet it paves the way for the return of timelessness and love's awakening, for fear must slip away under the gentle remedy it brings.

Forgiveness is the home of miracles. The eyes of Christ deliver them to all they look upon in mercy and in love. Perception stands corrected in His sight, and what was meant to curse has come to bless. Each lily of forgiveness offers all the world the silent miracle of love. And each is laid before the Word of God, upon the universal altar to Creator and creation in the light of perfect purity and endless joy.[166]

14. WHAT AM I?

I am God's Son, complete and healed and whole, shining in the reflection of His Love. In me is His creation sanctified and guaranteed eternal life. In me is love perfected, fear impossible, and joy established without opposite. I am the holy home of God Himself. I am the Heaven where His Love resides. I am His holy Sinlessness Itself, for in my purity abides His Own.

We are the bringers of salvation. We accept our part as saviors of the world, which through our joint forgiveness is redeemed. And this, our gift, is therefore given us. We look on everyone as brother, and perceive all things as kindly and as good. We do not seek a function that is past the gate of Heaven. Knowledge will return when we have done our part. We are concerned only with giving welcome to the truth.

We are the holy messengers of God who speak for Him, and carrying His Word to everyone whom He has sent to us, we learn that it is written on our hearts. And thus our minds are changed about the aim for which we came, and which we seek to serve. We bring glad tidings to the Son of God, who thought he suffered. Now is he redeemed. And as he sees the gate of Heaven stand open before him, he will enter in and disappear into the Heart of God.[167]

WORKBOOK EPILOGUE

This course is a beginning, not an end. Your Friend [the Holy Spirit] goes with you. You are not alone. No one who calls on Him can call in vain. Whatever troubles you, be certain that He has the answer, and will gladly give it to you, if you simply turn to Him and ask it of Him. He will not withhold all answers that you need for anything that seems to trouble you. He knows the way to solve all problems, and resolve all doubts. His certainty is yours. You need but ask it of Him, and it will be given you.[168]

What Are the Unique
Ideas in the Course?

≈ ◦ ≈

The direct quotations in the previous section gave the answers to fourteen questions and provided a summary of the Course in six pages. The three pages in this section provide an even briefer summary of the Course by answering the question, "What are the Unique Ideas in the Course?" The Course expresses many ideas that are not found in other spiritual philosophies of either the East or the West. Below are fourteen examples of these distinctive spiritual principles:

1. In order to remain the Lord of Love, God could not and did not create *maya* (the dream or illusions of this world). The dream of this world is not *lila* (divine play) because it was not created by God. Rather, you and all of your brothers and sisters made this dream, which could be called the "collusion illusion." This dream seems to be real because it is a *collective dream* rather than an individual dream that you have when you go to sleep at night.

2. You can only be where God has placed you. Thus you and all your brothers and sisters have never left Heaven. That is where you still are, while you remain sleeping in your dreams of separation from the Oneness of Reality.

3. Reality consists of "qualified nondualism." (Total nondualism is the belief that you lose your individual identity when you become aware of your Oneness with the All.) The Course's qualified nondualism consists of the paradox that each individual seeker is *part* of Christ and the *whole* of Christ at the same time.

4. There is cause and effect, but there is no karma as it is commonly understood in the East. Karma only seems to exist because of your illusory belief in the reality of guilt, which is a false and self-imposed belief in the necessity of self-punishment. Salvation is merely the complete release from the belief in guilt and the acceptance of holiness leading to the acceptance of reality.

5. All problems are solved in the *miracle* of the "holy instant" in which you become aware of your oneness with all of your brothers and sisters in the One Christ. The holy instant is only an instant in time, yet it is a window to the timeless eternity of Heaven.

6. The Course uses the term "revelation" to describe enlightenment, saying it is God communicating Himself directly to you and is not reciprocal (not you communicating yourself to God). Miracles are more useful now than revelation because of their interpersonal nature, connecting you with your brothers and sisters in Christ.

7. Jesus is your awakened elder brother and your equal in Christ, so Jesus is not more loved by God than you are loved by God. If you are open to the guidance of Jesus, he can assist you to become what he is now by helping you to wake up.

8. The Holy Spirit was created by God specifically for the purpose of helping all seekers to wake up from their self-imposed dream. He offers healing to their minds that have been split between one part that is committed to the truth and reality and the other part that is committed to falsehoods and illusions. Before healing the split mind with the *One-mindedness* of the Holy Spirit, you need to first let go of the ego's *wrong-mindedness* of false perceptions and accept the *right-mindedness* of true perceptions.

9. Every seeker has all the qualities of God with the following one exception: The seeker can never be the First Cause, which belongs only to God the Father. You cannot wake up from your dream by denying that God is your Creator, your Father. The dream of this world is an illusory and futile attempt to "create yourself" and make God Fatherless. The Course refutes this by asserting, "I am not a body. I am free. I am still as God created me."

10. What are called "sins" are merely mistakes that can easily be corrected. God created you by extending Himself into you so you are forever part of Him and cannot be defiled. Thus no mistake (often wrongly identified as a sin) can ever take away your perfect holiness that God gave you when He created you. The Holy Spirit's plan of salvation is called the *Atonement*. It is a plan of perfect love that has corrected all of your mistakes and their effects. But your responsibility as a miracle worker is to accept the Atonement in the holy instant and heal your own mind as you extend healing to others.

11. You have a burning love for God, just as God loves you completely. God's love for you and your passionate love for Him are hidden. You have lost your awareness of this love, but your lack of awareness has in no way limited the purity or reality of this all-consuming love still in your mind. The Holy Spirit separates all your fearful, false perceptions from all your loving, true perceptions. The Holy Spirit saves all your loving thoughts, called the "blessed residue," and He will bring this content of love with you when you finally wake up in your true Home in Heaven.

12. You can use Christ's vision—use the "eyes of Christ" or the "eyes of forgiveness"—to see the world light up figuratively and perhaps at times literally. You cannot wake up from the nightmares of your dream world and go directly to Heaven. Yet you can make the transition possible by first seeing the dream world as a "happy dream" ("real world") and later seeing the "face of Christ." You, your brother, and the world are always forgiven for what never happened. The happy dream is still an illusion, but it is an illusion of forgiveness that leads to awakening. Yet God must take the final step to bring about your awakening in Heaven.

13. Other philosophies apply generalization in only a limited way so learning is extended to *some* new situations as an option. The Course asks you to generalize your learning to *all* new situations as a necessity. For instance, you learn to forgive one person and one object in the world, in order to eventually learn to forgive everyone and all objects in the world, forgiving the world itself. If you leave anyone outside of your forgiveness, you will not be able to forgive yourself. Similarly, if you do not learn to love everyone, you will not be able to accept love as your own true nature, and you will not understand the true universal nature of love itself.

14. Other philosophies define terms by their distinct differences, just as the world makes comparisons and distinctions based on separating ideas. The aim of the Course is to reverse the thinking of the world and undo all you have taught yourself. The Course defines its terms by demonstrating how spiritual principles overlap, are interrelated, and have the same purpose and meaning of oneness. One holy instant contains all holy instants. One instant in time contains all the billions of years of time itself. One miracle contains all miracles. One true perception perfectly unified will unify all perceptions and lead to full awakening. How all true perceptions are unified in oneness is best expressed in this quotation: "Forgiveness, salvation, Atonement, true perception, all are one. They are the one beginning, with the end to lead to oneness far beyond themselves."[169]

What's Next?

~ o ~

Let's suppose you have read this overview of the Course and are intrigued by some of the ideas presented here. Possibly you may even want to consider the option of becoming a Course student. There are three reasons why you might want to know more about the Course:

1. You realize the need for a new and better thought system.
2. You begin to recognize the value of the Course principles.
3. You are willing to pay the price in time and effort to study the Course.

Hopefully this brief overview will help you to take the next step of studying the Course in more depth. Perhaps you are ready to read and study the 669 pages of the Text and the 92 pages of the Manual, as well as complete the 365 daily lessons contained in the 488 pages of the Workbook.

However, taking the step of studying the whole Course is quite a big price to pay. What if you are not yet ready to make this kind of extensive commitment to the Course? There is an intermediate step you can take that will put you in a better position to decide if you want to complete the entire Course. This intermediate option is provided by the book titled *The Two-Month Bridge to "A Course in Miracles."*[170] The subtitle is *A Condensed Edition of "A Course in Miracles*. This book is designed to be read after you have completed reading this overview. Since most beginners are reluctant to read and study the whole 1249 pages of the Course, this book offers a lesser commitment that requires only two months of study and application.

This two-month period can help you in two ways: If you are having trouble understanding the Course, you can acquire greater insight into its spiritual principles. If you are not yet convinced of the benefits of the Course, you can gain learning that will demonstrate the value of the Course. In particular, you can learn how to apply its lessons to your personal relationships. The first month is devoted to increasing your awareness of the spiritual principles in the Course. The second month focuses on the practical application of spiritual principles to your daily life. *The Two-Month Bridge to "A Course in Miracles"* provides guidelines for studying and applying the Course during the two-month training period. On the next page, you will find a brief description of some of the guidelines in this book:

THE TWO-MONTH BRIDGE

The Two-Month Bridge to "A Course in Miracles" is a study guide that helps you to make the transition from being a somewhat skeptical beginner to a committed Course student. It provides you with an intermediate level of training that utilizes a condensed version of the Course. The following is a summary of the two primary aspects of the Two-Month Bridge:

For the first month, you will read about the Course principles. *A Condensed Edition of "A Course in Miracles"* is the subtitle since this study guide contains an abbreviated version of the Course. It has the same words used in the full Course, but less essential and repetitious parts have been deleted for the sake of simplicity. This prevents the beginning student from being overwhelmed by receiving too much nonessential information all at once.

During the second month, you have the opportunity to apply the spiritual principles you have learned during the first month by doing thirty of the 365 daily Workbook lessons. The thirty lessons selected for this training period will expose you to a variety of spiritual experiences that will help you identify with your true nature as a spiritual being created by God, your Father Who loves you. Some of these lessons encourage you to develop your inner attunement, but the majority of these lessons are designed to foster healthy personal relationships based on loving forgiveness. This two-month training period will help you to evaluate the challenges and the benefits of incorporating spiritual principles into your daily life.

Although this book contains an abbreviated edition of the Course along with guidelines for how to use it for a two-month period, this study guide is certainly not a substitute for studying the full version of the Course. In fact, the Two-Month Bridge is called a "bridge" because it provides a temporary training period that bridges the gap between an old way of thinking and a new way of thinking. This "bridge in perception" serves as a steppingstone that prepares you for studying and applying the entire Course. The task of completing the 1249 pages of the Course seems less intimidating once a seeker has completed the lesser task of the Two-Month Bridge. The Course is not for everyone, but you won't know if it's right for you unless you explore some of what it has to say and have some experience of applying its principles. *The Two-Month Bridge to "A Course in Miracles"* offers this opportunity to become familiar with the Course and helps you decide if it's the right philosophy for you to believe, to study in more depth, and to apply to your daily life.

Performing a $5-Miracle

~ o ~

I first experienced a "$5-miracle" in 1980. I was in a restaurant with friends when a young man came over to our table and handed me a five dollar bill, saying, "This is for you."

I asked, "Why are you giving this to me?"

"It makes me happy to give it to you, and I see from your smile, it makes you happy to receive it. I don't need any other reason." Without waiting for a response from me, he turned around and walked away. At the time it seemed he had lost five dollars and I had gained five dollars. But many years later I would learn that we had both gained by an exchange of light and love and neither of us had lost. This experience was an example of what the Course calls a "miracle."

Let's suppose you have spent five dollars to purchase this overview of the Course and after reading it, you have opened your mind to the possibility of a new way of perceiving yourself and the world. Would this qualify as a miracle, which always involves a change in perception? It's almost a miracle, but not quite. If your positive change in perception ends with you alone, it would not be a miracle, since miracles are always interpersonal, including an extension of light and love from one person to another. A change in your personal perception becomes a miracle as soon as you let your opening to love extend to another person.

If you have read this overview and felt you have benefitted by it, I propose that you perform a simple "$5-miracle" by giving this book to a friend as a gift. Giving this gift will be a miracle as long as you give it as an expression of love, and your friend receives it as an expression of love, whether or not your friend accepts the ideas in the book.

I have priced this book at $5 so Course students can reasonably afford to give several copies to their interested friends. My purpose is to share with others the inspirational "gold" I have discovered in the Course. Right after I became a Course student, I was so enthusiastic that I made the mistake of trying to convince others to study the Course. I quickly discovered that most people like their own current thought system, and they don't want to change to a new way of perceiving themselves and the world. Also, most people don't want to take the time or make the effort to learn all about the Course. I did find some friends who were willing to listen to some of the ideas in the Course if I would explain them briefly. But I soon found out that the spiritual principles of the Course are so all-encompassing and unusual that they are hard to explain in a concise manner. Now I can just hand my friends a copy of this overview to introduce them to the Course, if they are curious about its spiritual principles. Some friends just want to know why I am so enamored with the Course. Other friends have studied the Course but still don't understand it, so this overview provides them with a solid framework for a better comprehension of the Course.

After a friend first introduced me to the Course, it took more than seven years before I finally made the decision to accept the Course as my thought system. Remembering those seven years of rejecting the Course prevents me from assuming that my friends will suddenly accept the Course. Those who need the Course will be attracted to it—sooner or later—and those who do not need it will not be attracted to it.

A realistic goal for me is to simply—to the best of my ability—be an example of applying the Course principles to my daily life. Most of all, I want to remain open to the new lessons the Holy Spirit wants to teach me every day. After all, the Course is not an end; it is just one way to continue a lifelong journey of discovery. Whether we study the Course or follow some other path, our various journeys are all leading to waking up in our Home in Heaven where we are joined in Oneness.

---

1. T-In.1, p. 1
2. T-24.In.1, p. 499
3. W-rV.in.5:4, 6:1-3, p. 330
4. W-in.8:1-6, 9:1-5, p. 2
5. T-14.VII.7:5, p. 289
6. T-26.I.1:7-8, p. 542
7. T-31.V.2:4-9, 3:1-4, 4:1-4, p. 656
8. W-93.1:1-3, p. 93
9. W-93.3:3, p. 161
10. T-31.VIII.6:1, p. 667
11. W-93.7:17, p. 162
12. T-7.I.3:3-6, p. 112
13. W-127.1:1-7, 2:1, p. 230
14. W-132.5:3, p. 242
15. T-6.II.8:1-5, 9:1-2, p. 97
16. T-11.VI.10:5-6, p. 209
17. T-13.VIII.2:1-5, p. 258
18. T-8.VIII.1:10-15, p. 155
19. T-23.II.19:1-9, pp. 493-494
20. T-13.III.10:2-5, p. 244
21. T-6.IV.2:1-5, p. 100
22. T-8.I.2:2-4, p. 138
23. T-5.III.7:1-7, 8:1-6, p. 79
24. T-5.III.9:3, p. 80
25. T-3.V.10:3, p. 46
26. T-14.VII.4:3-10, pp. 287-288

27. T-14.VII.7:1-11, p. 288
28. T-18.IV.4:1, p. 381
29. T-21.II.2:1-7, 3:1-3, p. 448
30. T-3.IV.4:1-4, p. 42
31. T-25.IX.10:6, p. 540
32. T-7.VI.4:6-7, p. 124
33. T-14.IV.3:4-8, p. 279
34. T-9.IV.5:3-6, p. 169
35. W-134.3:2, p. 248
36. W-134.4:1-2, p. 248
37. T-9.IV.4:4-6, p. 169
38. T-3.V.9:1, p. 46
39. T-31.VII.12:6, p. 665
40. W-30.2:1-5, p. 47
41. T-12.VI.4:4-10, p. 228
42. T-4.II.10:1-5, p. 59
43. T-12.VI.5:9, 6:1-7, 7:1-7, pp. 228-229
44. T-in.1:1-8, 2:1-4, p. 1
45. M-23.2:4-8, p. 58
46. T-1.II.4:3-6, p. 8
47. T-26.IX.2:2, p. 561
48. T-30.V.7:1-8, pp. 636-637
49. T-19.IV.D.3:4, p. 420
50. T-18.IX.10:1-7, pp. 395-396
51. W-pII.8.4:1-2, p. 443
52. W-pII.8.5:4, p. 443
53. T-18.VII.4:7-11, p. 389
54. T-18.VII.7:1-9, 8:1-5, p. 390
55. M-23.4:1-5, p. 58
56. T-16.V.6:5, p. 342
57. T-2.III.3:3-7, pp. 21-22
58. T-6.I.2:4-5, p. 91
59. W-in.8:1-6, p. 2
60. T-13.III.2:2, p. 242
61. T-13.III.4:1-5, p. 243
62. T-13.III.5:1, p. 243
63. M-13.7:7-9, p. 34
64. M-1.1:1-2, p. 3
65. M-1.4:1, p. 3
66. M-1.4:2, p. 3
67. M-1.3:5, p. 3
68. W-in.6:2, p. 1
69. W-in.5:1-3, p. 1
70. T-12.VIII.7:8-9, 8:1-9, p. 235
71. M-18.4:1-10, p. 48
72. M-22.3:1, p. 55
73. M-22.4:5-9, 5:1-10, 6:1-2, p. 56
74. M-22.2:1-5, p. 55

75. M-15.1:11-12, 2:1-7, p. 38
76. M-15.1:4-5, p. 38
77. T-2.VI.7:6-8, p. 30
78. T-14.VII.7:5-8, p. 289
79. M-7.2:1, p. 22
80. T-27.V.6:5-6, p. 578
81. T-12.II.3:5-6, p. 218
82. M-22.1:1, p. 55
83. T-13.VIII.5:4-5, p. 259
84. W-137.5:2-3, p. 261
85. T-27.II.5:2, p. 569
86. T-27.V.6:1, p. 577
87. T-22.VI.4:4, p. 481
88. T-5.II.1:2, p. 75
89. T-2.V.4:5, p. 25
90. T-27.II.4:1, p. 569
91. M-22.1:9, p. 55
92. M-22.1:3, p. 55
93. T-6.V.B.9:1, p.108
94. W-342.1:8, p. 474
95. W-67.4:3, p. 113
96. T-18.VI.11:4-11, 12:1-5, p. 387
97. T-15.V.10:8 -10, p. 314
98. T-18.VI.13:2-6, pp. 387-388
99. T-2.V.6:3-6, p. 26
100. T-21.I.8:1-5, 9:1-4, p. 447
101. W-108.5:1, p. 195
102. W-108.1:3-5, 2:1-3, 3:1-3, p.195
103. T-25.VI.3:1, p. 529
104. W-108.7:5, p. 196
105. T-7.XI.5:1-2, p. 137
106. T-9.V.7:2-9, p. 172
107. T-9.V.6:5, p. 172
108. T-2.VI.9:14, p. 31
109. T-8.III.1:3, p. 141
110. T-11.III.4:6-7, p. 199
111. T-7.III.5:1, p. 117
112. T-11.in.3:1-7, p. 193
113. W-15.3:1-7, p. 25
114. C-in.2:5-6, p. 77
115. C-4.3:6-7, p. 85
116. M-22.1:3, p. 55
117. T-3.I.6:5-6, p. 37
118. T-2,III.1:1, p. 21
119. T-2.II.6:9-10, p. 20
120. T-5.I.6:5, p. 74
121. T-14.VIII.2:13, p. 290
122. T-14.VI.2:1, p. 285

123. C-6.1:4-5, p. 89
124. C-6.3:5, p. 89
125. T-6.V.4:6-7, p. 104
126. C-6.3:4, p. 89
127. T-13.V.8:1-9, 9:1-8, 10:1-6, 11:1-7, p. 249-250
128. T-19.IV.D.2:3, p. 420
129. T-25.I.4:4-5, p. 519
130. C-4.7:1-7, p. 86
131. T-1.II.2:7, p. 7
132. M-26.3:1, p. 64
133. M-26.3:4, p. 64
134. T-3.III.5:10, p. 41
135. T-3.IV.7:4, p. 43
136. T-5.III.5:5-6, p. 79
137. T-1.II.2:5, p. 7
138. T-1.II.1:4-6, p. 7
139. W-28.5:1-2, p. 43
140. W-161.9:3, p. 305
141. T-17.II.1:1-9, 2:1-3. p. 352
142. T-2.V.9:4, p. 27
143. W-121.11:2-4, 12:1-3, 13:1-3, pp. 215-216
144. T-2.V.10:1, p. 27
145. T-27.VII.15:1-6, 16:3-4, p. 585
146. T-5.III.3:5, p. 78
147. W-357.1:2, p. 483
148. T-13.X.11:1-5, p. 265
149. M-4.X.2.7-13, p. 16
150. W-62.5:2-3, p. 104
151. T-1.I.45:1-2, p. 6
152. T-4.VI.6:2-3, p. 68
153. T-11.III.3:1-7, p. 199
154. W-pII.1.1:1-7, p. 401
155. W-pII.2.1:1-4, 2:1-5, p. 407
156. W-pII.3.1:1-5, 2:1-7, p. 413
157. W-pII.4.3:1-4, 4:1-4, p. 419
158. W-pII.5.3:1-5, 4:1-5, 5:1-8, p. 425
159. W-pII.6.1:1-5, 2:1-5, p. 431
160. W-pII.7.1:1-5, 2:1-4, p. 437
161. W-pII.8.1:1-4, 4:1-3, 5:1-4, p. 443
162. W-pII.9.1:1-3, 4:1-4, p. 449
163. W-pII.10.3:1-2, 5:1-3, p. 455
164. W-pII.11.3:1-3, 4:1-6, 5:1-2, p. 46
165. W-pII.12.2:1-5, 5:1-2, p. 467
166. W-pII.13.1:1-6, 3:1-5, p. 473
167. W-pII.14.1:1-6, 3:1-7, 5:1-5, p. 479
168. W.ep.1:1-9, p. 487
169. C-4:6-7, p. 85
170. Donald James Giacobbe, author; Miracle Yoga Services—pub. date: 2011